Big Book of GARAGES

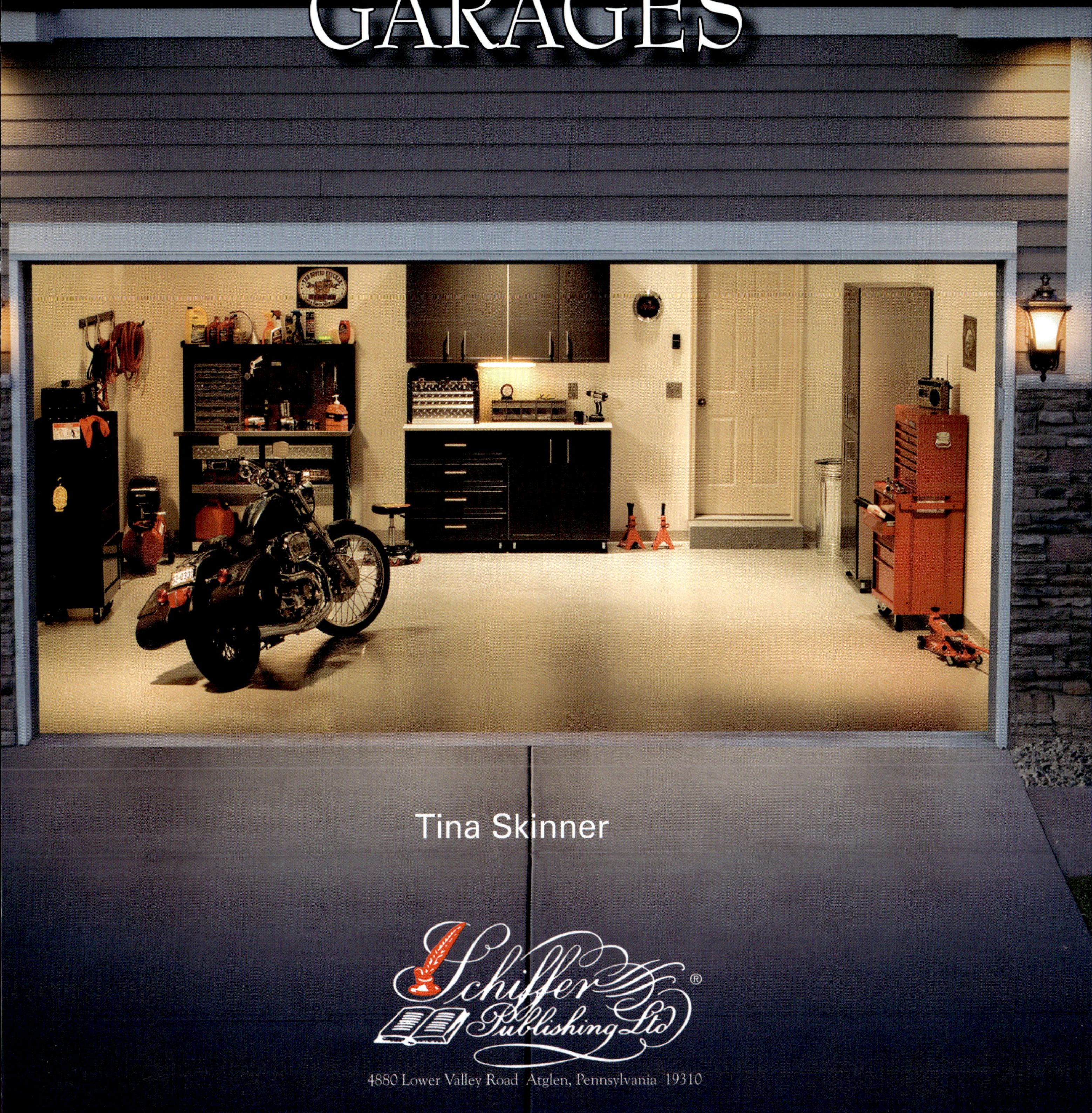

Tina Skinner

4880 Lower Valley Road Atglen, Pennsylvania 19310

Other Schiffer Books by Tina Skinner

Decorating with Concrete: Indoors: Fireplaces, Floors, Countertops, & More. Tina Skinner & the ConcreteNetwork.com ISBN: 0764322001. $19.95.
Hardscaping with Decorative Concrete. Tina Skinner. ISBN: 0764325981. $19.95.
Room by Room. Tina Skinner & Tony Hanslin. ISBN: 0764320068. $19.95.
Walkways & Drives: Design Ideas for Making Grand Entrances. Tina Skinner. ISBN: 0764313606. $19.95.

Other Schiffer Books on Related Subjects
Yesterday's Structures: Today's Homes. Lucy D. Rosenfeld. ISBN: 0764310143. $39.95.

Library of Congress Control Number: 2008935456

Photo Editor, Ginger Doyle
Research and Writing, Calvin Woodring
Text Editor: Jeff Snyder

Designed by "Sue"
Type set in Bernhard Modern BT/Zurich BT

ISBN: 978-0-7643-3155-8
Printed in China

Published by Schiffer Publishing Ltd.
4880 Lower Valley Road
Atglen, PA 19310
Phone: (610) 593-1777; Fax: (610) 593-2002
E-mail: Info@schifferbooks.com

In Europe, Schiffer books are distributed by
Bushwood Books
6 Marksbury Ave.
Kew Gardens
Surrey TW9 4JF England
Phone: 44 (0) 20 8392-8585; Fax: 44 (0) 20 8392-9876
E-mail: info@bushwoodbooks.co.uk
Website: www.bushwoodbooks.co.uk
Free postage in the U.K., Europe; air mail at cost.

Contents

Acknowledgments

With special thanks to Doug Bannister of One Day Floors, a division of The Stamp Store, for spurring this project on. He was very generous with resources and time in helping to demonstrate the latest technology in concrete micro-toppings. Additionally, brothers Joe and Jerry Sheehan and Tim Frazier of One Day Floors were inspiring in their passion for the perfect floor.

Additionally, one of the pioneers of garage cabinetry shared his enthusiasm and expertise for the subject. Many thanks to Don Mitchell of Cooper Garage Cabinet Systems.

Special thanks to Mischel Shonberg of Clopay Building Products and Jim Braxmeier, owner of Vanguard Doors Sales & Service, for images, door installation demo, and a wealth of information to be found on their website, clopaydoor.com.

Introduction

An open garage may not reflect the way people live beyond the front door, but it certainly provides a first impression. *Courtesy of Rust-Oleum*

With most American homes, the first thing you see as you turn into the driveway is the garage. If the garage door happens to be open, what greets you might be quite shocking. With the exception of all but the most fastidious of neat freaks, the garage tends to act as an overflow basin from the home. All sorts of odds and ends – the holiday stuff, the home improvement leftovers, the toys, and the someday donations to the Goodwill trickle into this space originally intended as a place to park the car. There's a reason those big bargain events are called "garage sales."

Here's a typical family garage. The inhabitants have attempted to organize a lifetime of accumulated stuff with shelving and containers. However, the whole system is doomed to ugliness simply because the walls and ceiling were never painted. *Courtesy of Garage Design Source*

Most homes have a garage, according to studies by the National Association of Home Builders and data from the U.S. Census Bureau. In 1950, 53 percent of new homes were built without a garage. An estimated 41 percent included a one-car garage, while 6 percent had a single carport. By 2004, the number of new homes with a single-car garage was a mere 17 percent, probably because 83 percent claimed a two-car or larger garage. The percentage

Another garage that might be on your block, this one was slowly filled with storage items, neatly piled so that humans could wend their way through in search of that occasional something. A car could never get through the mess. Everything had to be moved out in order to make way for the renovation. *Courtesy of Garage Design Source*

Even a brand new family garage has issues, with only a few spare boxes left over from the move in. Like most new construction, the garage was hardly considered. The walls were never painted and the floor is raw concrete ready to soak up oil and any other stain that comes its way. *Courtesy of Garage Design Source*

Garages Are Growing

While the average lot size for new homes has decreased from 10,000 square feet in 1990 to 8,500 square feet, the average size of the garage is growing. This is largely because the cars have grown. The standard size of the garage door has grown from 7 by 9 feet to 8 by 10 feet for a two-car garage bay to accommodate today's larger sports utility vehicles. Today builders are advised to allow 12 feet of width per vehicle and a depth of at least 24 feet.

of new homes with garages built for three or more cars has doubled from 10 percent in 1991 to 20 percent in 2005.

The three-car garage consistently receives high marks from consumers when asked to list their preferences for new-home features and amenities. The percentage of new homes with a three-car garage has doubled since 1991. For high-end buyers, storage requirements often exceed that.

Your intention in buying this book may simply be a desire to find room in the garage for the car once again. After your home, that car is probably your second largest investment. Moreover, with rising fuel costs, incidences of fuel theft and other burglaries are on the rise. A car is simply safer locked up inside. Some insurance companies even offer a discount for cars that are stored inside.

It's also going to last longer. Shielding your car from the elements will prolong its life. Sun fades the paint as well as interior surfaces. In the winter, that road salt that builds up on your car will melt off in the garage rather than stay frozen to the undercarriage and paint until the weather changes. Because it's warmer in the winter and cooler in the summer, your car is a lot more pleasant to climb into, too. Ice won't need to be scraped off the windshield, pollen won't coat it in the spring, and birds won't be able to use your car for target practice.

"America is a funny place," says Marc A. Shuman, president and founder of GarageTek. "We will keep an $80,000 Mercedes in the driveway in the weather and sun, and keep $5,000 worth of junk that nobody ever touches in the garage. GarageTek lets you bring your car back into the garage and put order to the rest of the stuff that's in there."

Besides making your car look better, a garage has a great deal of influence on the curb appeal of your home. Nice garage doors make a grand statement, and open garage doors offer the neighbors an eyeful. If you are concerned with improving that first impression for visitors, you want to work on ways to keep the garage tidy. Today's market offers all kinds of great storage systems that conceal clutter, organize tools, and keep the floor clear.

Like many homeowners, though, you may be thinking outside that box and envisioning a garage where there's a lot more going on than just parking things. The garage is bonus space just waiting to be claimed.

In researching the garage, we found that technology has moved ahead, and so have tastes when it comes to the home add-on that often sports unfinished drywall and a bare concrete floor. In many cases, people are transforming the garage into an extension of the home – using it as a mudroom, garden center, storing food there, and storing everything else from tools to sports equipment. The garage is often home to a workshop of some sort, be it woodworking or the mechanics of car maintenance. And in many cases, it's a place where people hang out. With the doors up, it's an indoor outdoor space where people can shelter from the hot sun while barbecuing nearby, a big open floor area where children can play, or the best open space where there's room to set up tables.

The best way to get started in transforming the garage from thoughtless add-on to proud addition generally begins with a complete overhaul. So rent a portable storage unit, haul out all that junk (and heave anything you don't want to haul back in). Pick a finish for your floors and walls, and invest in some cabinetry to hide the bulk of your clutter. Before you know it, you'll be on your way to owning a garage showplace.

In this book we'll explore options that start from the ground up, with flooring systems, wall and overhead storage ideas, and, to finish it all up, that all impressive first-impression door. We'll look at different uses you might put your garage to, in addition to, or instead of, automotive storage. Most importantly, we'll show you some of the best, professionally finished garages to be found today to inspire you.

Fun Fact

Many car insurance companies provide a 10 percent savings on an annual premium for parking a car in the garage; that's about $200 a year.
Source: *OrganizIT*

If you don't have a basement, or if you've added an addition, chances are the garage was elected as the place to keep a hot water heater. There are logical reasons for finding spaces outside the living areas of the home, most importantly the concern about malfunction. A leaking water tank causes far less damage in a garage. *Courtesy of OrganizIT*

Bare, stained concrete and unfinished walls characterized a garage that was given little love. In a dramatic makeover, the floor has been sealed and stylish cabinets installed. Painted walls and a slatwall system complete the new look. *Courtesy of Garage Finisher, Inc.*

BEFORE

BEFORE

AFTER

Remind you of your own garage? These homeowners tried to be tidy. They used bins and a homemade wooden shelf system to try to get stuff out of the way. Still, the inclusion of a cabinet system to hide most of the clutter, and slat wall systems to get stuff up and off the floor has made a world of difference. Children's play items are close at hand, and the newly refinished floor makes it easy to provide a clean, safe area indoors for the kids to get a little rowdy. *Courtesy of Garage Finisher, Inc.*

On average, the amount of clutter in this garage was minimal; it's just that it was all squished up against the far wall to make room for the cars. The environment was vastly improved by creating a cabinet system to organize and conceal everything. The old sink was replaced by a pretty one with countertop, and now the environment is so nice the owners are apt to use some of the space as a cozy front porch. And there is still room for the cars! *Courtesy of Garage Finisher, Inc.*

Opposite page:
A whole lot of stuff had to be carted out so the walls could be painted and new cabinets and slatwall systems installed. With everything back, and organized, it has made a world of difference. *Courtesy of Garage Finisher, Inc.*

BEFORE

AFTER

What We Do In Our Garages

The Hewlett Packard Company got its start in a detached garage in Palo Alto, now a historic landmark and the "Birthplace of Silicon Valley." Other mega-million-dollar businesses birthed behind big carport doors included the magazine *Reader's Digest*, Apple Computer, Liquid Paper, and the 1948 toy store sensation Wham-O.

Then there were the countless bands and top-hit singles that got their start in this room furthest from indulgent parents' sensitive ears.

For some, the garage has been a place of great inspiration, or industry. For most of us, though, it's just another place to keep the many needs and accessories of of everyday suburban life. The following images offer a tour of some of the uses garages find themselves tasked with, and offer up tidy ideas for your own storage solutions.

Garden tools and accessories are perfect candidates for garage storage. Although this is a fastidious gardener's work area, the fact is that garden work involves soil. *Courtesy of Garage Tek*

Big tools for yard and garden work are logical candidates for garage storage. *Courtesy of OrganizIT*

Sports equipment is ready at hand if properly stored in the garage. Moreover, if you have a "no throwing balls in the house" rule, the bin by the door helps reinforce it. *Courtesy of OrganizIT*

Bicycles are but another form of vehicle. They obviously belong in the garage. *Courtesy of OrganizIT*

Vehicles for each member of the family are lined up at the ready and out of the way. *Courtesy of OrganizIT*

Surfboards are ungainly items to store. This one finds its home high and dry. *Courtesy of OrganizIT*

Another mode of transport is kept safe in a garage. *Courtesy of OrganizIT*

Below:
A single-car garage is packed with storage, almost floor to ceiling. Space below the cabinetry leaves clean up an easier job. *Courtesy of Garage Design Source*

This showplace garage became the family's favorite "outdoor room" when kitchen appliances were added. Beverages are at the ready, and the table is the perfect place to linger, whether there is food on it or not. *Courtesy of One Day Floors*

A garage opens out to a barbecue area – the perfect gathering spot for a neighborhood get-together. *Courtesy of Garage Den*

Custom screens keep the bugs out of the food and create a huge screened "porch" area for a party. *Courtesy of Fresh Air Screens*

Bar stools and a table stake out hang-out space in a spiffy garage. *Courtesy of Garage Design Source*

Below:
A family spreads out in a three-bay garage. For children, the garage is a safe place to practice bicycling skills and to work out energy that would be frustrated inside. *Courtesy of Garage Den*

A screen keeps the bugs at bay while children enjoy an indoor-outdoor room. *Courtesy of Fresh Air Screens*

Children's bulky car seats hang above dad's golf clubs, both at the ready when it's time to load up. *Courtesy of OrganizIT*

A home office tucks neatly between the water heater and sports equipment. *Courtesy of OrganizIT*

If you're hanging out in the garage, you may as well watch a little TV. *Courtesy of OrganizIT*

Pets find their place in a garage, too. *Courtesy of OrganizIT*

What other room in the home is as easily cleared out for a big gathering? Simply back out the cars and then set up! *Courtesy of Gregory Montillo*

Formerly a garage, this homeowner opted for a home spa instead. Garage doors were replaced with privacy screens and a stone fireplace, and a whirlpool tub was parked here instead of the family car. *Courtesy of Aquatic Industries, Inc.*

Another adaptive reuse of a garage might include a home gym. The car can park outside this room, instead of the local YMCA. *Courtesy of Gregory Montillo*

In this case, the home's HVAC system and water heating system shares space with the family car.
Courtesy of Versatile Building Products, Inc.

Elements of the Garage

Doors

Today's garage doors are embellished with embossed and stained glass, wrought iron, and wood textures and finish that are nothing short of stunning. The trend is toward the "carriage door" look, with looks-only handles and hinges that create a French door look for a hinged unit that actually rises.

Investment in nice garage doors is touted as a major home upgrade, and smiled upon by realtors espousing the value of "curb appeal." Since most garages face the street to save on paved driveway, garage doors are one of the predominant features of the home. Surprisingly, few but the most upscale builders give them a lot of consideration, making upgrades the responsibility of the homeowner.

Even a nice paint job can bring new life to an aging garage door, of course. Inside, however, your garage space can be greatly enhanced with the addition of light-inviting windows.

Stained glass teams with wrought iron handles and hinges to create a coach house door straight out of the rich Victorian era. This door lifts up, however, and admits far more horsepower. *Courtesy of Clopay Building Products*

The temperature indoors will be greatly affected by the door, too. When shopping for a door, two important factors are insulation and the steel gauge. The lower the number, the stronger the gauge of the steel. If you might have basketball's hitting your garage door, you'll want a lower number/heavier gauge of steel, like 24. If you plan on spending a lot of time in your garage, have a room above or adjacent to your garage, or have a lot of activity, such as children playing, you want to consider the R-Value and the thickness of the door. R-Value is a measurement of the thermal efficiency of a door. The higher the R-Value, the better insulated the door.

Wrought iron adds both security and beauty to arched glass windows crowning these beautiful garage entry doors. *Courtesy of Clopay Building Products*

Genuine wrought iron hardware is a popular add-on for today's garage doors. Although not functional, these pieces are high in impact. Jim Braxmeier, owner of Vanguard Doors Sales & Service in Pennsburg, Pennsylvania, holds up two "handle" options for a Coachman-style door from Clopay. The decision made, it's as simple as screwing the handles on.

The following images from Clopay Building Products illustrate the dramatic makeover effect new garage doors can have.

Before & After

Before & After

Before & After

Before & After

Before & After

Before & After

BEFORE

AFTER

Before & After

Know Your Garage Door

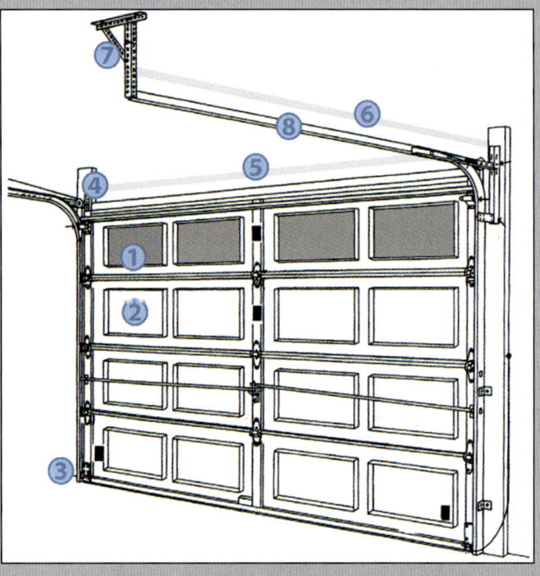

Courtesy of Clopay Building Products

1. Window Lite: Glazed section with various types of glass or clear acrylic to allow for light and visibility.
2. Sections: Panels reinforced with stiles interconnected with hinges and rollers.
3. Bottom Bracket: A structured support, which provides for attachment of lifting cables.
4. Cable Drum: Grooved drums on the torsion spring shaft that lifting cables wind around when the door is opening.
5. Torsion Springs: Provides the means to raise and lower the garage door via the cable winding on drums.
6. Extension: Extend along both horizontal tracks.
7. Rear Track Hanger: Suspends track from the ceiling.
8. Track: Provides a guide for section to raise or lower the garage door. Special tracks can be purchased for garages with low headroom. Vertical Track runs on either side of the opening. Horizontal Track is attached to ceiling. The two are connected by a curved track.

Chances are, you're not going to see a lot of glamorous garages in most parts of town. Here's a drive-by tour of some real stunners that will inspire you to outdo everyone else on the block. These doors do multiply – once one homeowner installs a stunning door, neighbors are often quick to follow suit.

You'll want to choose a door that fits your home's style. As far as color goes, these are usually applied by the homeowner or the installer and the options are nearly as endless as the color swatches at the paint store. Still, there are special considerations to take into account when painting a garage door, and the manufacturer should be contacted for recommendations and warnings. Some colors or kinds of paints may impact your warranty on a new door.

Opposite page:
Double doors, side-by-side, reflect the symmetry of the roofline. Transom-like windows admit light, while preserving privacy within. *Courtesy of Jeld-Wen Windows & Doors*

Two garage doors carry on the window treatments from the front of the home, their structure and paint pattern mimicking the mullions. *Courtesy of Clopay Building Products*

Care & Maintenance

The normal functioning of the garage door is something we too often take for granted—until something goes wrong. Furthermore, because powerful springs are involved, a malfunction could result in injury or even death, marking one good reason to inspect your garage doors periodically. If signs of wear are observed and the proper steps are taken, homeowners can avoid costly accidents.

One of the first things to check is whether all of the components are securely fastened and working: hinges, springs, rollers, and any safety components. To test the springs, lift the door a few feet off the ground and then release it—if it moves a great deal in either direction, the springs are either worn out or improperly adjusted. A visual check of the springs should also yield some information. Are there signs of deformation, such as kinks, gaps, or bends? If so, it may be time to replace your springs, and, unless you're certain you know what you're doing, it's usually best to call a professional door technician. High-tension mechanics have the potential to inflict serious injury when tampered with.

For this reason, all garage door springs should be equipped with safety cables that run through their coils, in case of failure; if the movement of the spring is restricted, it is much less likely to cause damage in a malfunction. When inspecting your garage door, check to see that your springs are equipped with safety cables. If so, inspect them for signs of wear (frayed ends, for example). If cables are not installed, they should be. Again, as a general rule, if in doubt, call a professional!

Check the door tracks to see if they are plumb and level, and parallel with the door itself. The screws that hold these tracks in place are key; replace them if they show signs of rust or deterioration.

Newer automatic garage doors have an infrared sensor to stop them from closing and reverse their direction if something is in the way (e.g. your foot, your car, your dog). In some cases, these devices

Windows highlight the arched auto entryways to this home, their beauty accented in a contrasting color to the stone surround. *Courtesy of Clopay Building Products*

Below:
Arched windows on the garage doors carry on the arched forms of the picture window above and the towering front entryway. *Courtesy of Clopay Building Products*

can be lifesaving. Check the sensor on your garage door frequently to make sure it is functioning properly. When installing a new door, make sure the sensor is no more than six inches from the floor of the garage, to ensure that pets or small children under the door will be detected.

Finally, lubricating all of the moving parts in your garage door will help keep it operating smoothly. Be sure to follow the manufacturer's instructions.

Fun Fact

Average garage size has almost doubled in the last two decades

60% increase in three car garages in the last decade.

Source: *OrganizIT*

Translucent doors admit light by day, and give off a glow at night, preserving privacy within. The frosty finish is perfect accompaniment to the home's contemporary wood-clad character. *Courtesy of Clopay Building Products*

A pergola adds architecture to an expansive double garage, while faux carriage doors below add character. *Courtesy of Clopay Building Products*

Painted cross beams create a sense that this was once a barn on a historic property. *Courtesy of Jeld-Wen Windows & Doors*

Red doors remind us of the old barn, and give the sense that cottage and carriage house were married on this charming lot. *Courtesy of Clopay Building Products*

Front door and garage entries were matched perfectly in wood and glass for a stunning stone home that demanded the very best. *Courtesy of Clopay Building Products*

Green doors swing up not out, but still one gets the sense that horses might emerge with carriages at any given moment. *Courtesy of Jeld-Wen Windows & Doors*

Custom doors grace a garage complex. *Courtesy of Clopay Building Products*

A plain saltbox home gets an upgrade with coach-house style doors capped by an arched row of windows. *Courtesy of Clopay Building Products*

Floors

The number one improvement you can undertake in transforming your garage is sealing off the concrete floor. Bare concrete is why your garage doesn't count as the "interior" of your home. Concrete breathes, and it gets wet. It can conduct water from the ground into the atmosphere of the garage, and it can allow liquids to penetrate and stain its surface. That's why garage floors always have that mottled appearance.

Moreover, being a porous surface, concrete is much more prone to wear and tear. Small stones, sand, and dirt that come in on your tires eat their way through the surface of the concrete. Once the surface is scratched, deterioration of the surface is accelerated, and chips and "spalling" begin.

For those storing cars in a garage, particularly antique cars and hobby cars that aren't used often, the life of the tire depends on having a good moisture barrier between the rubber and the cement. At the bare minimum, you're going to want to care for your concrete and maintain it.

If you're starting with fresh-poured concrete in a home of new construction, you're going to want to shop for a good sealer. Home improvement stores carry a variety of wonderful products that will help protect your floor and prolong its life. If you're starting with a floor that's already seen a lot of living, there are things you can do to help restore it.

Cracks in your garage floor, while not necessarily indicative of structural failure, are unsightly, and collect dirt and debris. This can make for a difficult time cleaning, and over time the cracks will expand to create bigger problems for homeowners. For this reason, it's a good idea to routinely inspect concrete floors and patch cracks and holes as they arise.

For cracks up to 1/8 of an inch wide, caulk or various kinds of cement sealants are the simplest solution—just make sure whatever product you use will adhere to any floor finish you plan to use after the repair.

As cracks increase in size, however, to between ½ an inch and 2 inches wide, concrete patching compound becomes a necessity. This is a dry product that you mix with water (or latex additive for increased strength and elasticity). Preparing the surface to be patched is essential for best results: the area around the crack should be scoured with a wire brush and cleaned of any dust and debris using muriatic acid to remove any oily residues.

Because the existing concrete can absorb moisture from the patch (compromising its strength), the area should be kept damp throughout the repair.

First, use a paintbrush, coat the inside of the crack with the patching mixture. Then, pour the mixture into the crack, filling about 1/3 of the space. Using a trowel, agitate the freshly poured patch, packing it in and removing air bubbles. Repeat this process until the patching compound fills the crack and extends beyond the rest of the surface. After waiting for 30-40 minutes, use the trowel to make the patch flush with the original surface. The patch should be allowed to cure for at least two days before sustaining vehicle traffic.

After repairs, the next step is to choose a finish.

Concrete Stains & Paints

There are a variety of great new concrete sealing products coming into the market with the expansion of the decorative concrete Industry. Masonry sealers are designed to penetrate the pores of the concrete for a waterproofing effect, and there are many that both stain and seal the concrete, creating a stronger surface and providing incredible visual effects. However, it's important to investigate these products, since many of them are so new. And it is really important to follow the manufacturer's instructions to ensure that the finish properly adheres and cures so that it will last. You can contact manufacturers and ask to see examples in your area that have undergone real-life conditions like vehicular traffic and spills. You will probably end up hiring an installer who has the proper equipment and experience to do the job right.

Courtesy of Versatile Building Products, Inc.

A specialty sealer, freshly applied, makes concrete glamorous. The nature of this wonderful material is allowed to shine through, with the control cracks for expansion dispelling any doubt that these are slabs of natural rock. A nice sealer, however, makes the floor shine, and makes it easier to clean and care for. *Courtesy of Versatile Building Products, Inc.*

Today's professionals in the concrete industry can provide stunning effects in concrete finishes. Here masking was used to create a two-tone floor that mimics tile. *Courtesy of Versatile Building Products, Inc.*

One option for the do-it-yourselfer is to use patio and porch enamel paint, which, although it allows for a greater range of color, possesses far less durability than epoxy finishes. For a slightly larger investment, Rust-Oleum has developed a kit for those who want to do their own work that mimics the look of a more expensive, professional epoxy or polyurea job. The EpoxyShield™ system is a quick and easy one-coat application specifically designed for concrete garage floors. It comes with two base tones and the option of including decorative paint chips for a look that imitates high-end coating systems on the market today.

Courtesy of Rust-Oleum

Next use the included concrete etch to thoroughly clean the surface. *Courtesy of Rust-Oleum*

To start, prepare the concrete area you will be coating. Sweep away any loose dirt or concrete chips that rest on the surface, patching areas that have spalled or cracked. Newly poured concrete should be allowed to set for 28 days before applying Epoxyshield. *Courtesy of Rust-Oleum*

Thoroughly stir the contents of each can (Parts A and B) before mixing them together. Before application, the combination should be mixed completely. *Courtesy of Rust-Oleum*

Because the Epoxyshield mixture dries quickly, it's helpful to have two people applying the coating. For corners and edges, use a small brush. Then use a paint roller and work in 4- by 4-foot areas, tossing the paint chips (if desired) onto each square as it is finished. These will be incorporated into the final product to produce a stunning effect. *Courtesy of Rust-Oleum*

After etching, rinse the area with water. Before the Epoxyshield coating can be applied, the concrete must be allowed to dry completely. *Courtesy of Rust-Oleum*

In 24 to 48 hours (depending on humidity and temperature), the surface should be ready for foot traffic. Vehicles should not be driven over the surface for seven days, until the mixture has completely cured. *Courtesy of Rust-Oleum*

Floor Tile Systems

There are a number of different application options for garages that a homeowner can easily undertake, such as tiling systems designed for quick and easy installation. In the case of interlocking aluminum or plastic tiles, you don't have any glues or fumes to worry about, and you don't need any tools. A single garage bay can be "repaved" in an hour or so, and the tiles can be picked up and move with you when you please. Most garages are level, but you'll want to be sure that yours doesn't have dips in it before you invest in tiles, though.

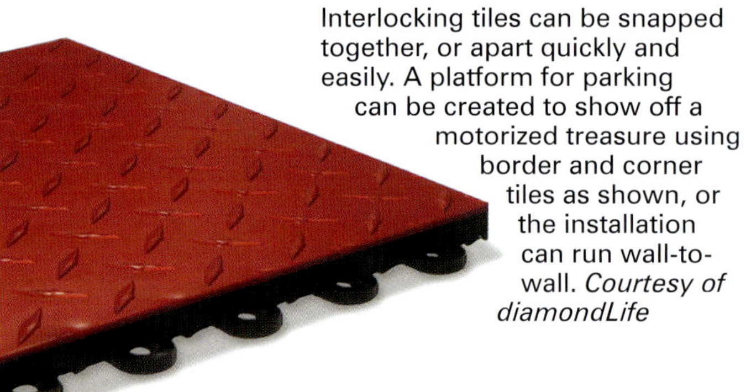

Interlocking tiles can be snapped together, or apart quickly and easily. A platform for parking can be created to show off a motorized treasure using border and corner tiles as shown, or the installation can run wall-to-wall. *Courtesy of diamondLife*

Garage carpeting is another option. Squares of indoor/outdoor carpeting can help hide unsightly stains, or protect a nice floor from leaks. Adhesive squares are a nice option that allows you to customize your colors and quickly create a floor that is friendly underfoot and eye-catching, and costs as little as $5 per square foot.

If you might consider a different system in the future, though, it's important to realize that extra cleaning, and possibly grinding, will be necessary to remove residual glues.

Self-adhering carpet squares specifically designed for garage use are built for heavy-duty wear and easy clean-up. TuffCarpet™ is created completely of synthetic polymer fibers made to feel soft and cushy rather than prickly. The result is a carpet that feels as good as it looks. The synthetic polymer fibers do not absorb liquids and so liquids evaporate away quickly. Spills can be scrubbed out with an oil cutting detergent and washed off. *Courtesy of diamondLife*

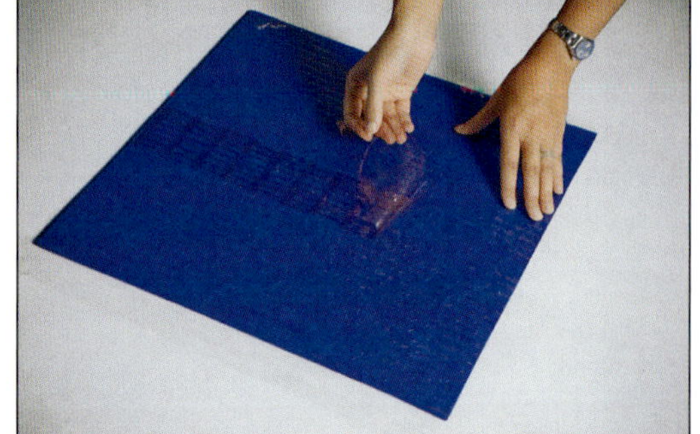

TuffCarpet™ squares have a bonding adhesive on the backside for easy peel and stick installation. A unique three liner system lets you expose only a narrow strip of adhesive for initial contact to the floor allowing you to fine tune the position before removing the other two liners and pressing the entire carpet square to the floor. If a carpet square gets damaged it can be peeled up and replaced. *Courtesy of diamondLife*

Bottom Line

GarageTek charges customers an average of $30 per square foot to revamp the garage. In comparison, it costs approximately $300-$400 per square foot for a major upscale kitchen or bath remodel.

Professional Coatings

At the top end of the market are the commercially applied epoxy and polyurea finishes that effectively bond with the concrete and seal the floor. These are manufactured and designed specifically for the garage market, and come in a variety of colors and finishes that are very attractive.

We photographed One Day Floors applying the latest technology to a garage floor, a coating that can be applied in all weather conditions, and a cure so fast it can be completed in one day. Recent developments with polyaspartic have resulted in an optically clear coating that needs only an hour or less between coats, even in low temperatures. The polyaspartic coating in One Day Floors delivers superior abrasion, chemical and UV resistance, and none of the hot-tire pick-up associated with other coating systems. A key ingredient in One Day Floors is the polyaspartic sealer, applied with three thin coats surrounding the colorful chips. One Day Floors is perfect for indoor or outdoor projects.

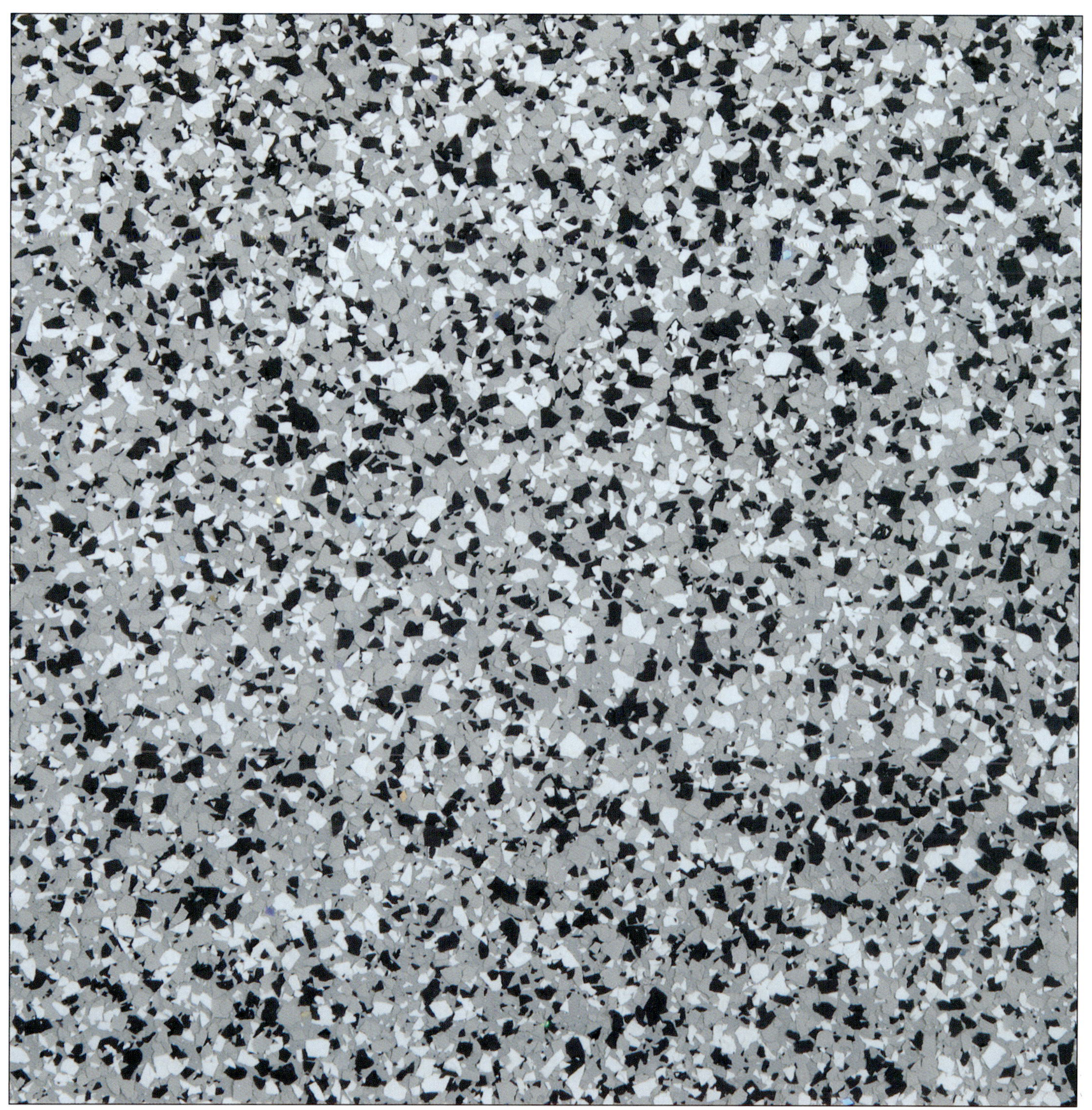

A detail of polyurea finish with grey tone color chips.

The floor is carefully sanded to remove all deposits and any sealer that was applied to the concrete previously.

Below:
The process of refinishing a floor begins with a diamond-bit grinder.

A hand grinder is used to finish the edges and any surfaces the floor grinder cannot reach.

The floor grinder collects the lion's share of the dust, cutting down on prep time.

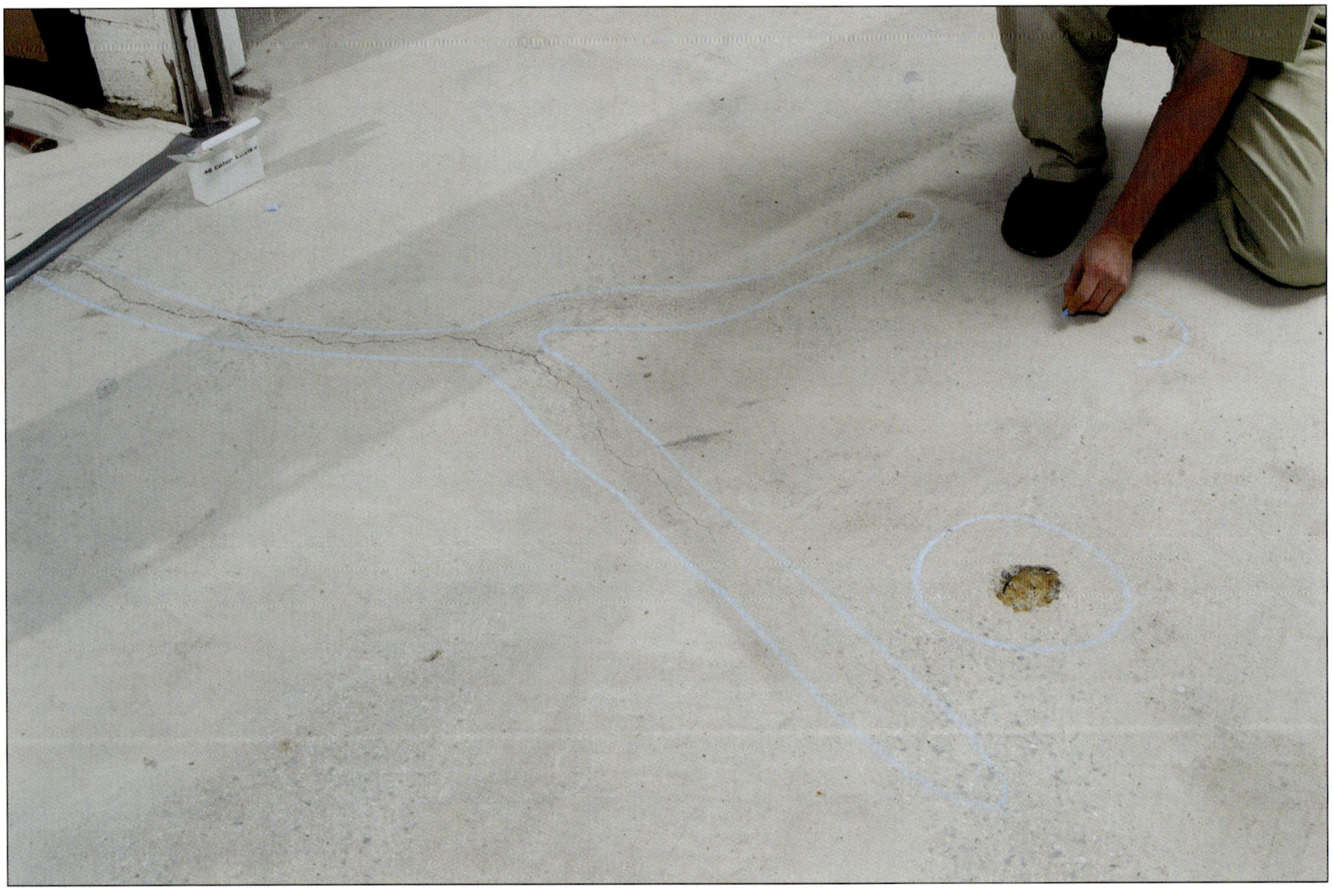

Cracks and chips are outlined in chalk. Often cracks are revealed after grinding. In the case of this floor, thin spots were found where concrete was poured over a surface that was not level.

A two-part sealer is mixed quickly...

... and poured into the cracks ...

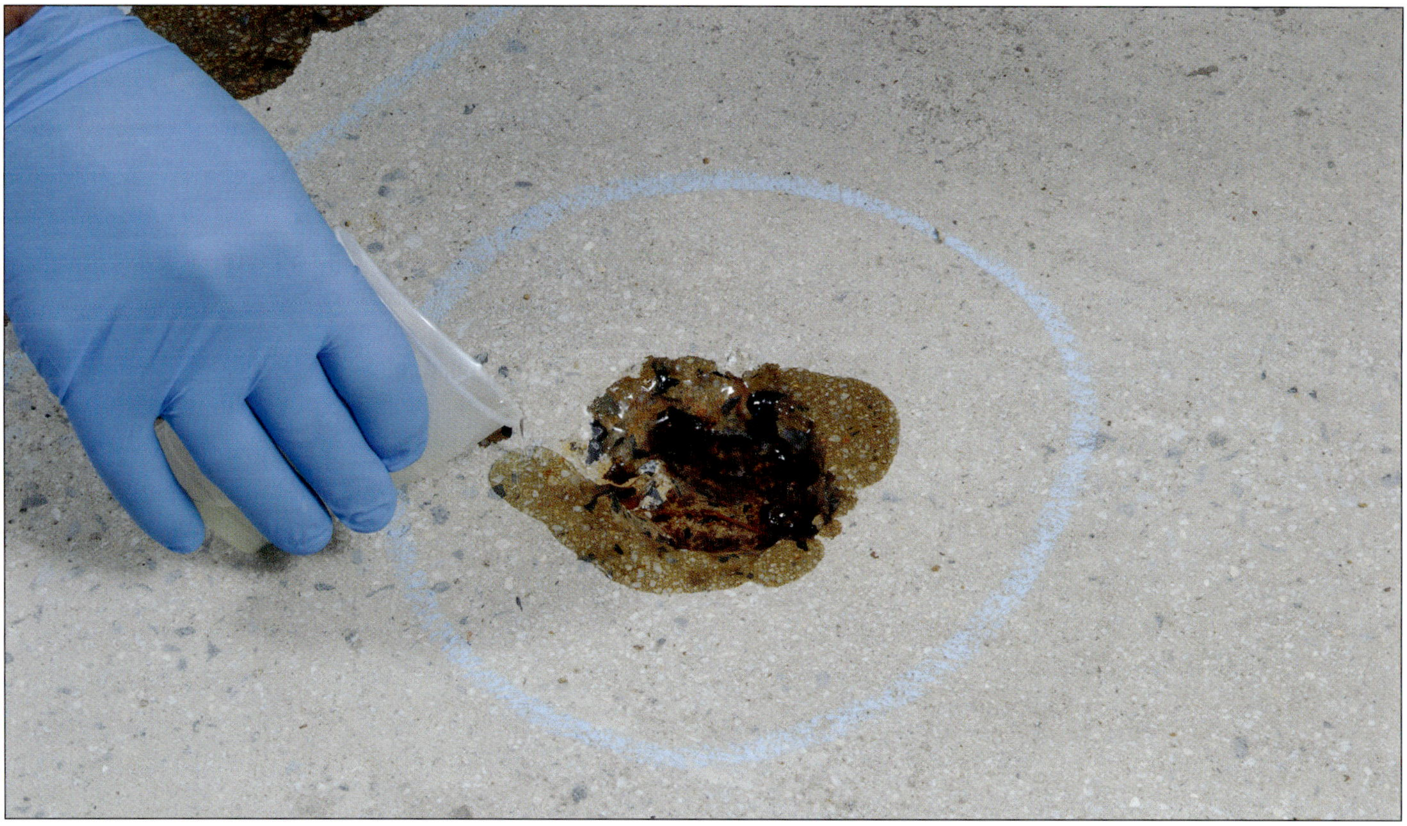

... and holes. This hole was actually a spot where the original concrete floor was poured micro thin over an unevenly excavated floor.

A blade is used to work the solution into the crack.

A hand grinder is used to level around the crack sealer after it has set.

The entire surface is carefully vacuumed before the first coat of the floor sealer is applied. Water is never applied to the concrete during the process so that it does not become trapped under the sealer.

The first coat of sealer is applied with the base color. While one man rolls it on the floor, another brushes it along the border. Each coat takes less than one hour to cure.

Color chips are pre-mixed. The process involves lots of buckets to facilitate the "fluffing" process. In this case, shiny chips are added to create a sparkle effect as the chips are first poured out of the manufacturer's box.

The chips are poured back and fourth between the buckets many times to fluff them.

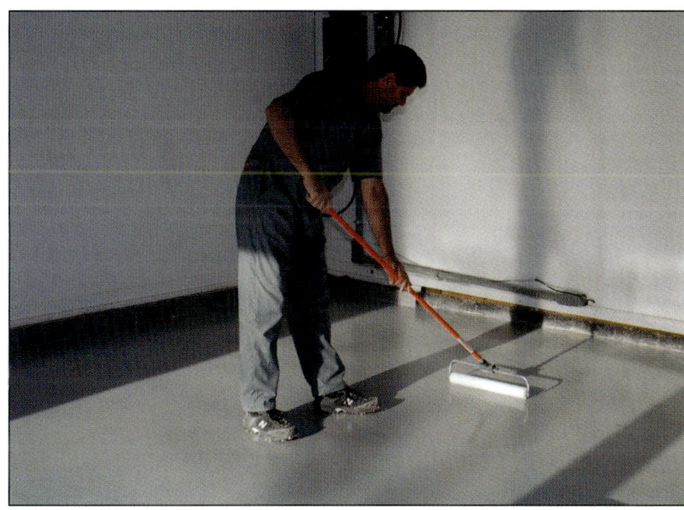

The second coat is applied as quickly as possible. In this case, two men worked on the border while another rolled the center of the floor.

While the second micro-coating is still wet, the color chips are broadcast. The process involves tossing the chips high in the air to help spread them widely.

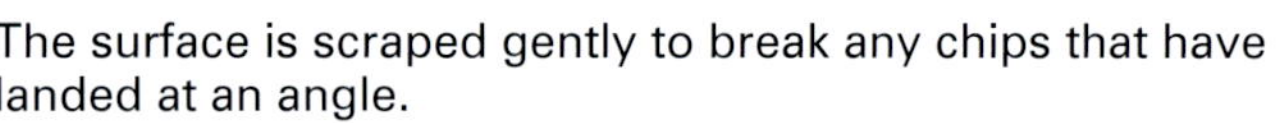

The surface is scraped gently to break any chips that have landed at an angle.

Broken and excess chips are vacuumed up.

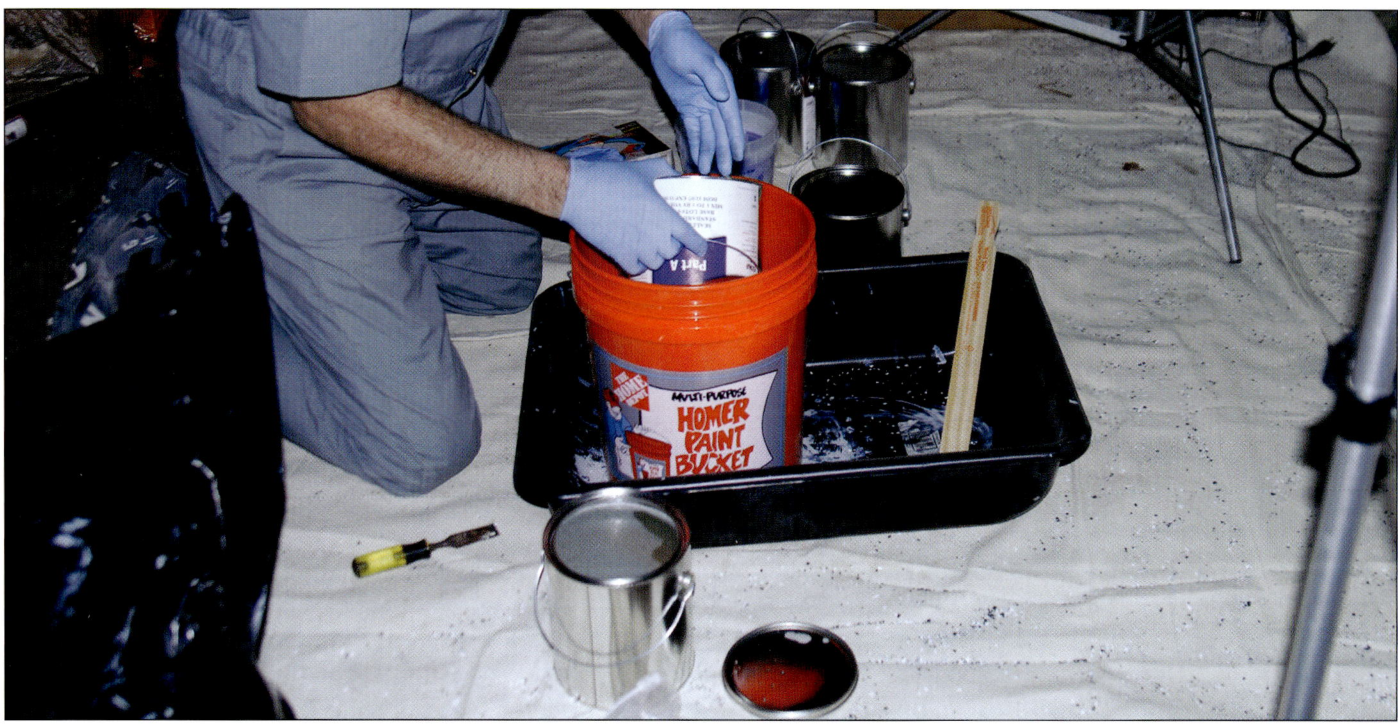

The final sealer is mixed, including a micro-abrasive that will provide traction in the final coating for safety...

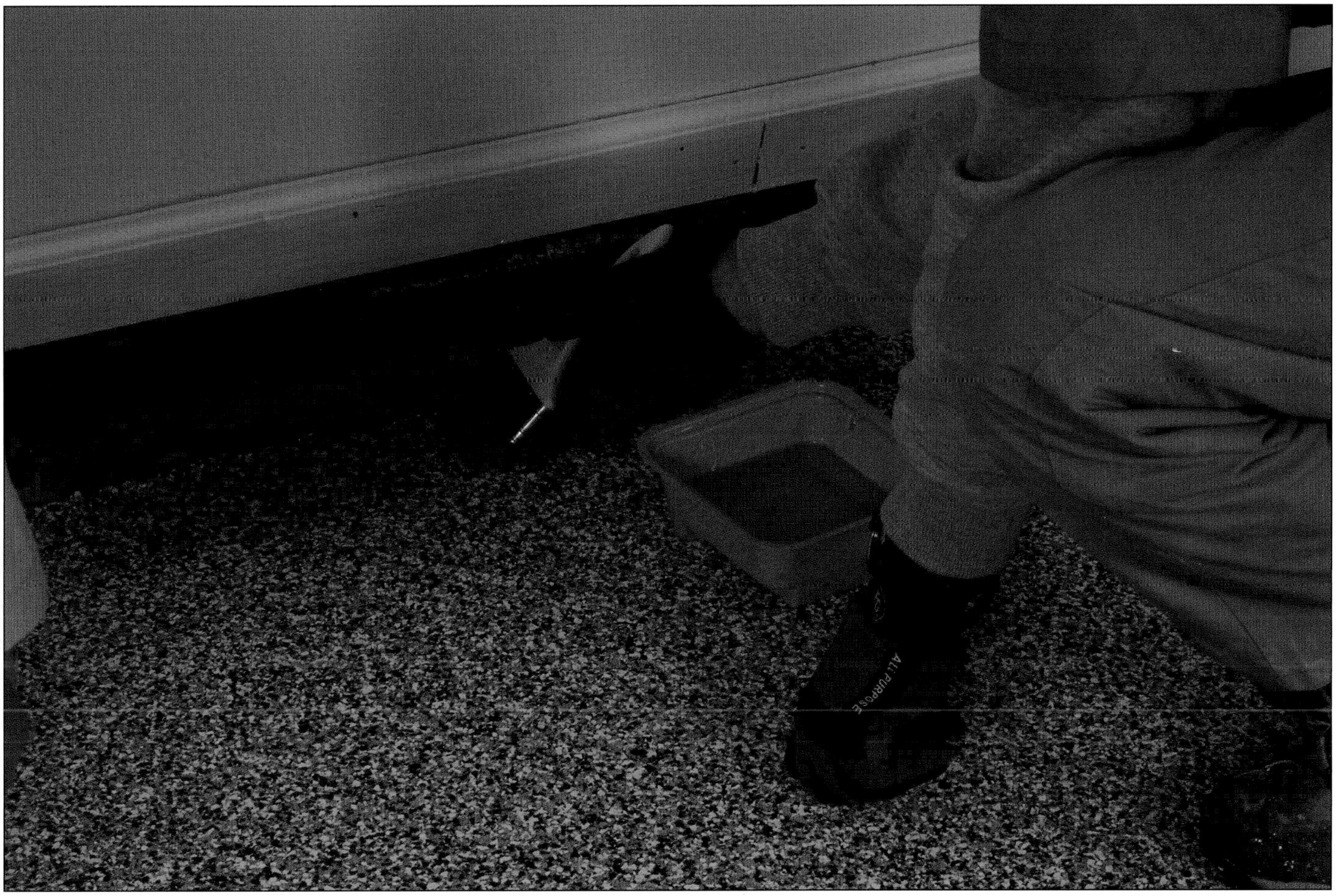

... and quickly brushed on around the edges. The gloves are worn because it was actually below freezing temperature as this floor is completed in the dead of winter.

Sealer is then poured along the back wall area of the garage...

... and is spread evenly with a squeegee across the floor.

As a final step, a roller helps to evenly distribute the last coat. Note the special shoes that strap on and allow the worker to walk on the finish without sticking to it or leaving tread tracks. The micro-abrasion, Sherwin-Williams' Sharksking, is a safety measure in a floor that is now perfectly smooth, faultless, and gleaming. It's finished in under a day, and ready to walk on in one hour.

Gorgeous Floors

Following are a few examples of fine floors for more inspiration.

In this one-day makeover project, the remainder of the afternoon is spent assembling storage units by Cooper Garage Cabinet Systems and installing them. The cabinet system is designed to hang from the walls, leaving clearance underneath that makes clean up easier, and prevents issues with moisture build-up and mold.

A chip finish in brown tones blends with wood-tone cabinetry. *Courtesy of PremierGarage*

A colorful floor is in keeping with two-tone cabinets for a race-track theme. *Courtesy of OrganizIT*

Below:
A single bay garage is ready for the owners to move back in. A three-tone floor will help guide them in parking, and a wall-mount system will make it easier to keep the area free for pedestrian passage. *Courtesy of Garage Design Source*

Decorative concrete sealers both protect and beautify a garage floor. *Courtesy of Garage Design Source*

Color adds excitement to a garage, setting the stage for its future as a play area for an active family. *Courtesy of OrganizIT*

A well sealed concrete floor is far easier to maintain than easily stained and scuffed bare concrete. *Courtesy of Versatile Building Products, Inc.*

Wall cabinets are raised above the floor to make cleaning a far more simple process in the future. *Courtesy of OrganizIT*

Perfect Parking

The sickening crunch of the front fender should never be the sound that welcomes you home upon driving into your garage. Yet most of us are familiar with the irritating and costly accident of pulling in just a hair too far and colliding with any number of objects: the lawnmower, the tool cabinet, the bike rack—maybe even the cement wall. In any case, the resulting dents and scrapes are a nuisance to fix, and often even more of a nuisance to explain ("No, dear, I didn't run over anyone on the way home..."). Equally common is the opposite mistake—failing to pull in far enough, and subsequently having your rear fender dinged by the garage door as it closes.

In ancient times, this dilemma was overcome through the clever use of a tennis ball suspended from the ceiling by a string. The garage owner would simply pull the vehicle into its appropriate space, then measure a length of string such that, when attached to the ceiling at one end and a tennis ball at the other, it would reach a point somewhere on the windshield of the car. That way, the next time the driver pulled into the garage, the tennis ball would lightly tap the windshield when the car was optimally positioned. (Other objects will do in a pinch, but can increase the risk of scuffing your windshield—every recorded attempt to use a shot put or bowling ball, for example, has ended in disaster.)

While this technique remains viable in the 21st century, it has a few inherent shortcomings, including the relative unsightliness of the contraption, and its inability to guide the lateral positioning of the car as it enters the garage. Especially where space is tight, and multiple vehicles park side by side, the danger of miscalculating and pulling in too far to one side is ever-present, and can result in a dented car door. Luckily, modern science has yielded a solution: laser-guided parking systems, which shine a beam from the ceiling to match up to an exact spot on your car every time, thus ensuring precision parking, no matter who's driving (parents: consider your newly licensed teenager). These systems are available in separate models for single-car and double-car garages.

Other options open to the peeved parker include simple parking mats that cradle your car's tires in the right place, or, when all else fails, bumper guards to install on the most frequently struck walls.

A self-adhering aluminum parking device can be positioned to guide your car into it's perfect parking position every time. *Courtesy of diamondLife*

Wall Systems

Today there are an infinite range of wall hanging systems on the market geared specifically for the garage. The systems are easily assembled, easy to clean, and easy to reorganize as your needs change. And they're stunning. Following are some stunners.

Pegboards

Back in the day, you bought pegboard and some hooks at the hardware store and you had storage. Your tools hung here, handy and ready. If you were smart and saved all those baby food jars when your family was starting out, you could stack them and you'd have the perfect way to organize those nuts, bolts, nails, and other little bits. It wasn't fancy, but it worked. The pegboard system has been vastly improved, both in terms of appearance and in the kinds of hardware you can use to accessorize.

A metal pegboard has added style made with commercial-grade diamond-plate. *Courtesy of diamondLife*

The old fashioned pegboard is still doing its job in grandpa's garage, as well as the slickest parking spots to be found. Here, metal pegboard and race-inspired textures dress up the look. *Courtesy of diamondLife*

An aluminum diamond plate pegboard with chrome-like luster is the ultra organizational center with wire baskets and hooks that make it easy to both organize and find things. *Courtesy of diamondLife*

A metal pegboard gets big tools off the ground, and the look coordinates with a shiny HVAC system in the corner. *Courtesy of diamondLife*

Slatwall Systems

One of the most popular upgrades for today's garage is finishing one or all the walls with a new slat system. The wall slat systems are designed to hold an impressive amount of weight, and come with a great variety of interchangeable hardware. Moreover, the finishes are easy to keep clean. Not only do you not have to paint your garage, you won't need to finish the drywall if you're installing wall slats.

A cross section shows the profile and strength of slat wall technology. *Courtesy of diamondLife*

Tools hang at the ready in an exquisitely organized mechanics garage. *Courtesy of Garage Design Source*

Shelving is suspended at the ready on a wall-mount system. *Courtesy of OrganizIT*

Below:
A wall mount system allows all the members of a busy family opportunities to put their things up and out of the way. *Courtesy of Garage Design Source*

A worktable provides the perfect home office, complete with a window view and a seat that rolls out of the way when the car rolls in. *Courtesy of Garage Den*

A feminine touch added color coordination to garage storage. A bench seat suspended on a slat wall is the perfect platform for taking off those work boots before entering the house. *Courtesy of Garage Tek*

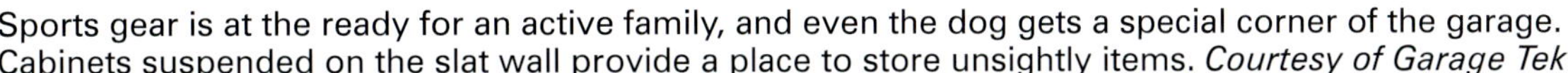

Sports gear is at the ready for an active family, and even the dog gets a special corner of the garage. Cabinets suspended on the slat wall provide a place to store unsightly items. *Courtesy of Garage Tek*

Wall storage can be accomplished via a variety of methods. Here the homeowners have opted for lots of hooks, and some shelves higher up. *Courtesy of OrganizIT*

Keeping the floor clear of items makes it much easier to clear the dirt and debris at cleaning time. *Courtesy of OrganizIT*

Grid Work

So simple in concept, so infinitely useful in so many ways, a metal grate can be paired with all manor of hardware for attractive wall storage.

A wire racking unit creates a visual statement while also providing a handy place to hang items at eye level. *Courtesy of PremierGarage*

Stainless steel racking is both attractive and rugged for garage storage. *Courtesy of diamondLife*

Cabinetry

Cabinets specifically designed for the garage are the honest trend in makeover improvements. Don Mitchell, who founded Cooper Cabinets and was an early leader in the industry, said one of the keys to his success was suspending the cabinets off the floor. By leaving the floor clear it made it easier to clean up a room that inevitably gets cluttered with dead leaves and soil that blow in through the big open doors via wind, tire treads, or car draft as vehicles enter and exit.

Cabinets for the garage have to be able to withstand temperature extremes, since garages are rarely heated or air-conditioned. They should have durable surfaces that are easily cleaned, since they are inevitably opened and closed by the dirty hands and gloves that are engaged in the messy work of auto and lawn maintenance. And they need to be built to handle heavy loads, since they are likely to store tools and equipment.

Fun Fact

Average self storage unit fee is $100+ a month for a 10ft X 10ft unit.
Source: *OrganizIT*

The best thing about garage cabinets, however, is that the doors close and hide all those items that really don't need to be on display. For one thing, it won't encourage robbers who peek through garage windows. For another, it simply looks better should the neighbors get a glimpse when the garage doors are flung open.

Grey cabinetry coordinates with the floor finish and provides a cool look for this recently remodeled garage. *Courtesy of Versatile Building Products, Inc.*

Flooring, cabinetry, and slatwall system provide a monotone background that will help subdue the inevitable onslaught of this-and-that soon to find a home in this garage. *Courtesy of OrganizIT*

Cabinets were hung high to conceal the seldom-used items of storage, while large, easily accessed sports and garden equipment are kept easily accessible. *Courtesy of OrganizIT*

Below:
Two tiers of cabinetry create an incredible bank of storage for this garage and prevent clutter from building up in an unsightly way. *Courtesy of OrganizIt*

Today's garage cabinetry has all the fine detail of units you'd hang in the kitchen with brushed metal hardware and wood-grain finishes among the many options. The cabinetry is designed, however, to withstand the swings in temperature associated with the garage environment. *Courtesy of PremierGarage*

A metallic finish is right at home in the automotive environment. *Courtesy of PremierGarage*

Varying cabinet sizes, styles, and display heights creates visual interest for a corner workshop area. *Courtesy of Garage Design Source*

Sparkling white finish provides an unexpected pristine background for the garage. *Courtesy of OrganizIT*

Base cabinets underline overhead storage systems. *Courtesy of OrganizIT*

Little Extras

Besides utility, a garage can have style. There are lots of new products coming online for the garage enthusiast, from specialty clocks and artwork, to special hardware. Here are a couple of ideas, and there are many more contained throughout the pages of this book.

Self-adhesive metallic molding adds style and quick cleanup to the garage. *Courtesy of diamondLife*

For even greater cleanup ease, self-adhesive wainscot tiles add racetrack style to the garage environment. *Courtesy of diamondLife*

Overhead Systems

The best way to get stuff off the floor is to lift it up. And leave it up!

All kinds of wonderful devices are being invented for getting stuff up high, where you can get to it when you want it, but otherwise keep it out of your hair. The garage ceiling is the perfect candidate for utilizing overhead space.

A simple pulley system hoists a big object up and out of the way. *Courtesy of Garage Design Source*

A hydraulic lift system raises loads well out of the way. *Courtesy of Garage Design Source*

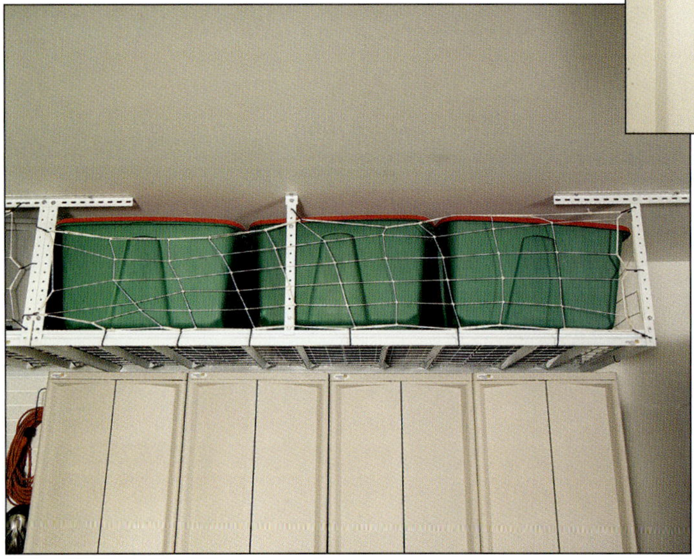

Large tubs are safely ensconced behind netting on a racking system suspended from the ceiling. *Courtesy of OrganizIT*

Built-in shelving creates an overhead library for stored items. *Courtesy of OrganizIT*

Cars Rule

Getting back to basics, let's take a look at garages as the place where we keep our cars. After your home, your car is probably your second largest capital expenditure. You may just want to protect it, or you may want to spend more time with it. In either case, let's look at how cars fit into some spectacular garages.

Mechanics' Mansions

If you are going to work on your car sometimes, you'll store your equipment in the garage. If you're going to work on your car all the time, here are some garages to emulate.

To stay out of the beating sun or the blinding rain, or simply to stay close to the tools, work on the car is logically done within the confines of the garage. *Courtesy of Rust-Oleum*

Dedicated to a beloved collection of Harley-Davidson motorcycles, this garage can entertain biker friends for hours. *Courtesy of One Day Floors*

Harley-Davidson is the theme here, too, with a colorful red motif to make sure the enthusiasm isn't missed. *Courtesy of Garage Design Source*

Fun Fact

25 percent of homeowners with garages do not use them to park their car, instead they hold clutter
Source: *OrganizIT*

An enviable tool locker stands at the back of a garage. *Courtesy of One Day Floors*

Temples to the Automobile

Here are samples of some truly wonderful garages, paying homage to the glory of the automobile.

Fun Fact

73 percent of Americans enter their home through their garage.
Source: *OrganizIT*

www.stevenholmesphotography.com

Interior designer Kerrie L. Kelly has a client with a Porsche collection that merited a designer garage. Glass and metal doors, brushed silver and carbon fiber cabinetry were combined with a killer paint scheme. In addition to the cars, the garage is home to a memorabilia/art collection commemorating Formula One races the owner has attended all over the world

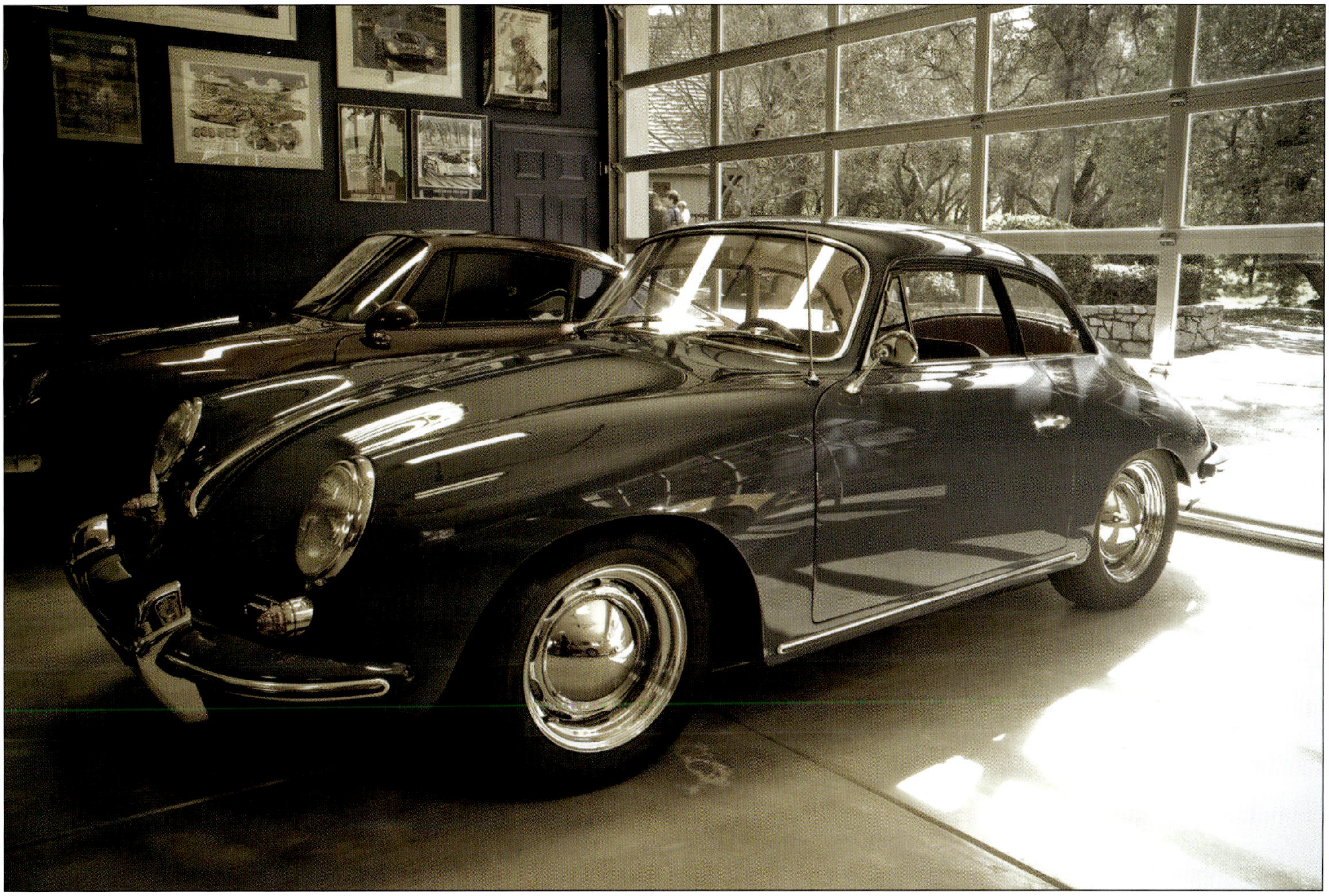

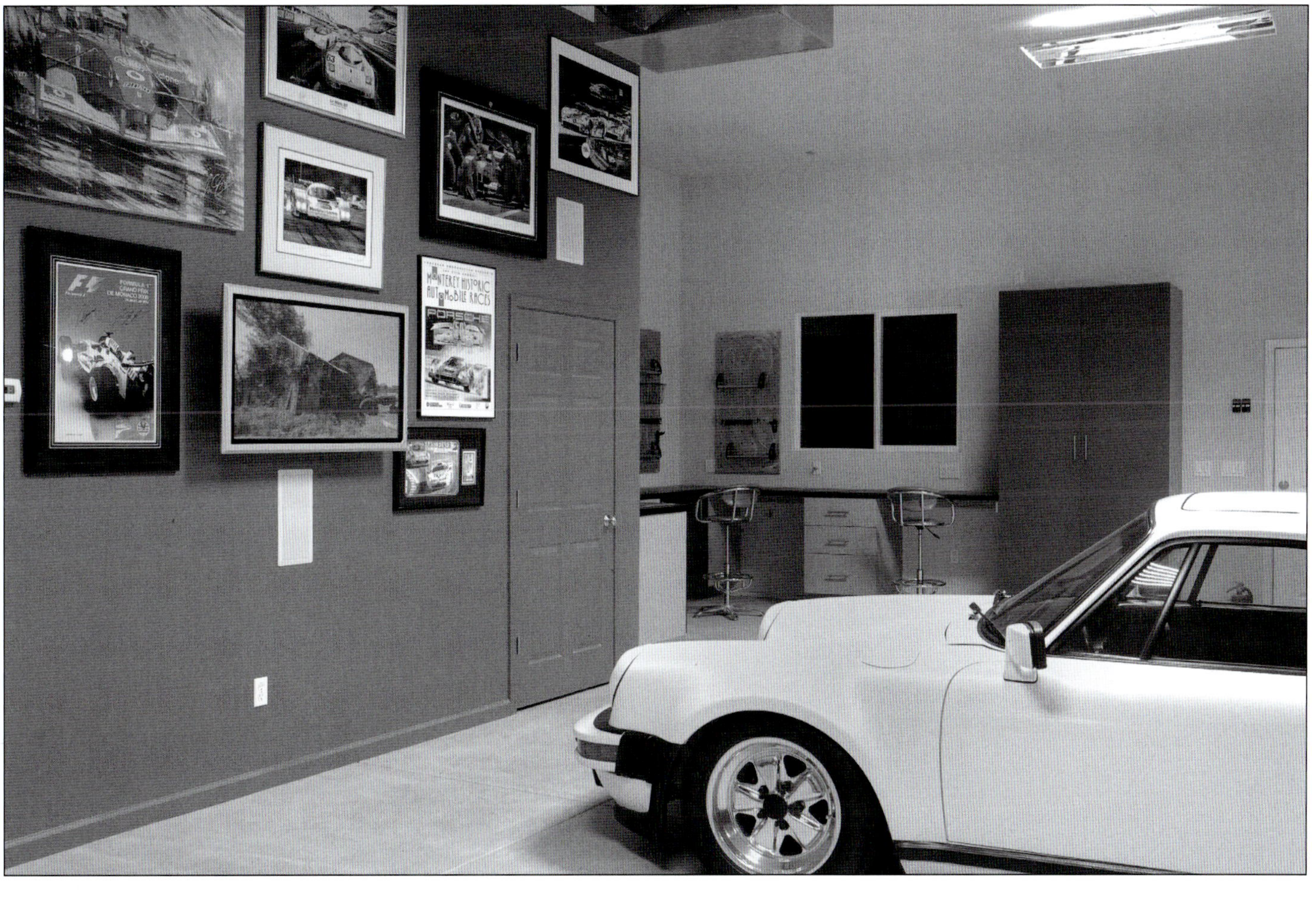
MONTEREY HISTORIC AUTOMOBILE RACES
PORSCHE

A prized possession enjoys a pristine environment. *Courtesy of Garage Design Source*

A biker's baby commands its own corner of the garage. *Courtesy of Garage Design Source*

Gallery of Great Garages

A single bay garage gets a makeover. Floor detailing adds a sense of space to the room, and wall storage adds utility to the small space. *Courtesy of Garage Design Source*

Don't Forget Your Car

A garage can become such a great place, you might decide you need it more than your car. However, even as cars become increasingly constructed of plastic and other non-metal materials, rust poses a serious threat to the longevity of your vehicle. At the very least, the frame of any given automobile is constructed of metal and susceptible to rust. Cars in coastal and northern areas are especially at risk. There are a few simple measures, however, which can protect your car from the elements and keep it rust free for years.

The most obvious of these measures is parking the vehicle in a garage. In places with high humidity, this will go a long way towards protecting the undercarriage and other areas of exposed metal, acting as a buffer layer against the environment. Likewise, subjection to large amounts of precipitation over a long period of time can cause rusting, another factor eliminated by the garage.

In coastal regions and places where roads are salted to combat ice and snow, drivers should take steps to wash their cars more frequently. Salt buildup can be corrosive to a car's finish, and result in increased rusting. A thorough cleaning and rinsing (taking care to completely rinse any exposed metal) every few weeks is essential to preserving the longevity of your vehicle.

Other easy steps to protecting your car from the elements include periodically waxing it, and checking under the interior carpet for moisture and signs of rust formation.

A fanciful mural references the "tiger under the hood" for a car enthusiast, and racing colors stake out the parking space. Cabinetry conceals the heaps of treasure that once cluttered this garage. *Courtesy of OrganizIT*

Earthen tones anchor this garage, and beige and white provide a light and airy atmosphere. *Courtesy of OrganizIT*

A polished wood floor and bold red cabinetry set this garage apart from the pack. Display cabinetry frames a collection of helmets, competing with a flat-screen television for attention. Even the powder room has pizzazz, with an automotive theme. *Courtesy of Architextures, LLC*

Prior to being stuffed with storage, an newly remodeled garage awaits boxes and bags to arrive to fill its shelves. *Courtesy of OrganizIT*

Purple and yellow are exciting colors to include in a garage. If you can't be fanciful here, then where? *Courtesy of OrganizIT*

Garages Rock On

Since its coinage, the term "garage band" has become an essential part of the American musical lexicon. Referring to groups of amateur musicians who ostensibly practice in their suburban garages, the phenomenon of garage music arose in the early 1960s, as American musicians attempted to reproduce the sounds of British pop, rock, and blues acts that were becoming popular on the radio. This was high-energy rock and roll at its gritty realest, and the passion, if not the skill, of its practitioners was never questionable.

In some instances, garage bands broke onto the airwaves to enjoy mainstream success, as was the case with the Kingsmen and their hit version of "Louie Louie" (featured prominently in the movie *Animal House*).

Most garage bands from this era remained in relative obscurity, however, save for the local popularity they often enjoyed. Among garage acts that received national airplay were such groups as Paul Revere and the Raiders, the Electric Prunes, the Seeds, MC5, and Question Mark and the Mysterians.

In the late '70s and into the '80s, garage music enjoyed a huge revival with the rise of punk music. Louder was better in this era, with groups like the Ramones rising from garage band obscurity to national fame. Among punk fans, some bands that never broke the surface of mainstream attention remain cult classics, including such acts as the Sonics, the Gories, the Dirtbombs, and Thee Mighty Caesars.

More recently, garage music has experienced a third renaissance with the popularity of such bands as the White Stripes, the Strokes, the Hives, and the Kings of Leon, to name a few. Eschewing big production values in favor of lo-fidelity, straightforward rock and roll, these groups aim to steer their brand of American music back to its roots in the garage.

Clearly a woman has taken over this corner of a garage. The space has been transformed into an attractive mudroom and potting center for an avid gardener. *Courtesy of Garage Finisher, Inc.*

A raised floor area at the back of a two-car garage is home to new cabinets and a workstation. *Courtesy of Garage Finisher, Inc.*

Opposite page:
White cabinetry and shelving create a cool, crisp look over a stunning purple floor. *Courtesy of OrganizIT*

Diagonal lines in flooring add a sense of spaciousness to this room. *Courtesy of Garage Den*

For most of us, coming home to clean and organized is a cure for stress. *Courtesy of PremierGarage*

Three parking bays sparkle in a cleanly white garage environment. *Courtesy of OrganzIT*

A plethora of family ephemera finds a home along the periphery of this garage, with just enough room to tuck in two cars and still find your way down the center aisle to the house. *Courtesy of OrganizIT*

Outdoor gear, a home office, and a treasured antique car coexist in a handsome garage. *Courtesy of PremierGarage*

A garage serves as entry to the home. It also has a refrigerator for food storage, and a washroom that allows the garage to be used as a mudroom. *Courtesy of OrganizIT*

Over the Top with GarageMahal

With the garage make-over market gaining ground in the home remodeling business, a lot of people are looking toward the future and innovating—none more so than Michael Rhodig of GarageMahals. He offers the following thoughts, with an apology that "It's more the rambling of a man driven mad by his passion for his work."

Creating the Ultimate Garage

By Michael Rhodig of GarageMahals

They say, and I like to quote, "Every dog has his day," and the day of the garage has come. If you look back at the history of residential development you'll see how the home has evolved in lockstep with its owner. Not all that long ago, indoor plumbing was virtually non-existent. Kitchens were little more than a wood stove and a tub for a sink. As for home entertainment systems of the past, you were your home's entertainment system.

All this has completely changed in the last 60 years or so. Particularly in the last 30 years. Now we have lavish kitchens of gleaming stainless steel on our patios—a far cry from the briquette barbecue of yesteryear. Home entertainment has gone from the black and white in the living room, to a theater in the home. The point is we can clearly follow the development of the home from room to room in our modern era of innovation. We have witnessed the maturation of each space to something far more luxurious and sophisticated, and now expected.

However, there is still one space that has not matured. It's typically the largest room in the home, and it is also the most neglected. Though it started as a barn, without improvement, the garage is no longer seen as even fit for the family pooch. Who would suffer their beloved pets to live in such a primitive environment? Never fear Fido, help is on the way. So much so that *you* may not be worthy of the garage.

It came to me as an epiphany, like many things do, that the garage could be so much more than it was, and I set out to create in my mind what it could be and how far I could take this concept. I understood then that the garage is "the final frontier of home improvement." Yes, I actually said that. You can ask my wife.

Now six years later, I have amazed even myself. From a creative designer's point of view, the garage is the perfect blank canvas. Everyone has been focusing so diligently on the rest of the home, this space is still wide open, and yet undefined. Yes there have been some innovations, but not much. The garage is still that place where we toss everything that lies in that wilderness between the living space and the trash can. It's largely a stop over for items we can't quite decide whether or not we should throw away.

If we haven't packed too many items in this limbo space, we might even be able to fit in a small car or two. Let's not forget, that was the original intent, at least on the architect's desk anyway. Of course we all know that current architectural standards for garage design don't really quite mesh with current standards for automobile design. These people need to start talking. You think? What I mean is, when was the last time you could put two cars in a standard two-car garage, and could actually get in and out of the thing without performing contortions that will later require chiropractic care? But, before I can move the mountain of architectural standards, I need to create demand.

My garage design work is founded on three simple principals:

1. The garage is a distinct space, and is not bound to traditional rules of design and use.
2. Everything has a place.
3. Nothing is seen, but what is meant to be seen.

These rules have led me to a wonderful place of creative innovation. I spent three years doing just research, looking at materials, getting samples, talking to reps, visiting manufacturers, and doing my own testing. My first GarageMahal was my own garage where I had complete creative license to do whatever I pleased. I cleaned it out completely, stood in the middle and said to myself, "Let's start from scratch." That was how it had to start. I had to dump all preconceived ideas about the space, like they were the stuff that got piled up in there over the years, that needed to go out to the trash.

Now, the garage is finally coming into its own. Because of rule #1, the garage can be a very exciting place. I'm not kidding. Not only will it hold some fantastic showpiece vehicles, but also it is a fantastic showpiece itself—a multifunctional space that is unlike any other in the home. Metallic surfaces, bold colors, unique fixtures, audiovisual entertainment, touchscreen controls, automated doors, and beer taps! Holy Moly, finally the answer to the question "Who is Batman?" is "I am Batman!" Only there are no bad guys to fight, and I don't have to keep this place a secret. The Joker and the Riddler are my buddies and hangout with me in my cave. That's why we have beer taps.

However, as much as this space is described as a "man cave" it usually appeals to everyone. When introduced to such a space I've witnessed equal reactions of wonderment and joy from both men and women and people from ages 5 to 75. And why not? Comparing what we expect a garage to be and what a GarageMahal is, is like comparing the city landfill and Disneyland.

My three simple rules change the way we see the garage. Rule # 2 puts an end to those nasty pegboard tool-hanging messes your grandfather used to have. You know, the ones with the outline of the tool. Okay, you can still have pegboard if you must, but it has to go inside a cabinet. Rule # 3 really creates some interesting thematic effects to hide the mechanical aspects of the rollup door. The combination of Rules 2 and 3 have got me to come up with some really awesome structures to conceal those hard-to-hide items like ladders, bicycles, and the folding ping pong table. Believe it or not, there really can be a place for everything. Of course, if you don't put it back where it belongs, that's your problem.

As with starting any business that cuts a new edge and has to define its own space, launching GarageMahals and forging off into that new frontier has been an exciting venture. It's like being a kid again and taking a ride on a giant roller coaster, a place in your heart and mind where fear, fun, laughter, and shear terror all share the same place at the same time. Like that kid on a coaster, I'm loving the ride.

Michael Rhodig imagines the garage in a whole new light.
Photography: www.jessemoen.com

A palatial garage in the Chicago area is a fantasy getaway for an auto-loving, fast-living homeowner. The Vegas theme is complete with magical lighting, and plenty of space to hang out. The project epitomizes Michael Rhodig's mission to re-create the garage, unrestricted by conventional notions of what the room should be. *Courtesy of GarageMahals.*

A bar and lounge area are among the amenities in the Vegas-themed garage. Colorful concrete finishes, innovative lighting, and a no-holds-barred approach are elemental to Michael Rhodig's garage designs. *Courtesy of GarageMahals*

TH

An Art Deco theme combines past design aesthetics with space-age lighting and technology. Glass windows flanking the grand pedestrian entry have been obscured for privacy. *Courtesy of GarageMahals*

A colorful floor motif seems to radiate up the walls and sculptural features of this metallic-finish environment. Stunning warm colors are artfully lit beneath a towering black ceiling. *Courtesy of GarageMahals*

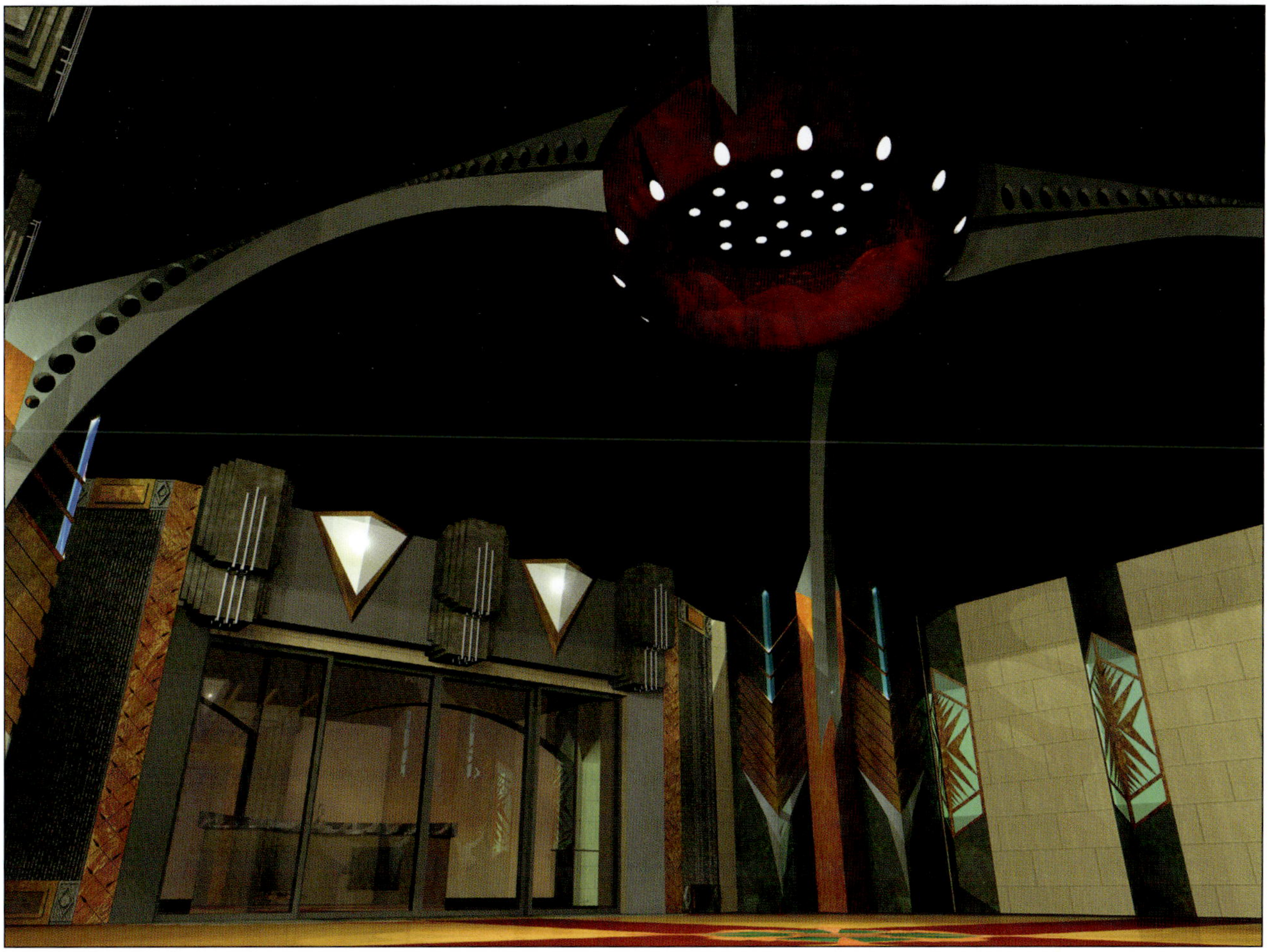

A circular bar culminates the expansive, four-bay garage. A rolling ladder provides access to overhead storage. *Courtesy of GarageMahals*

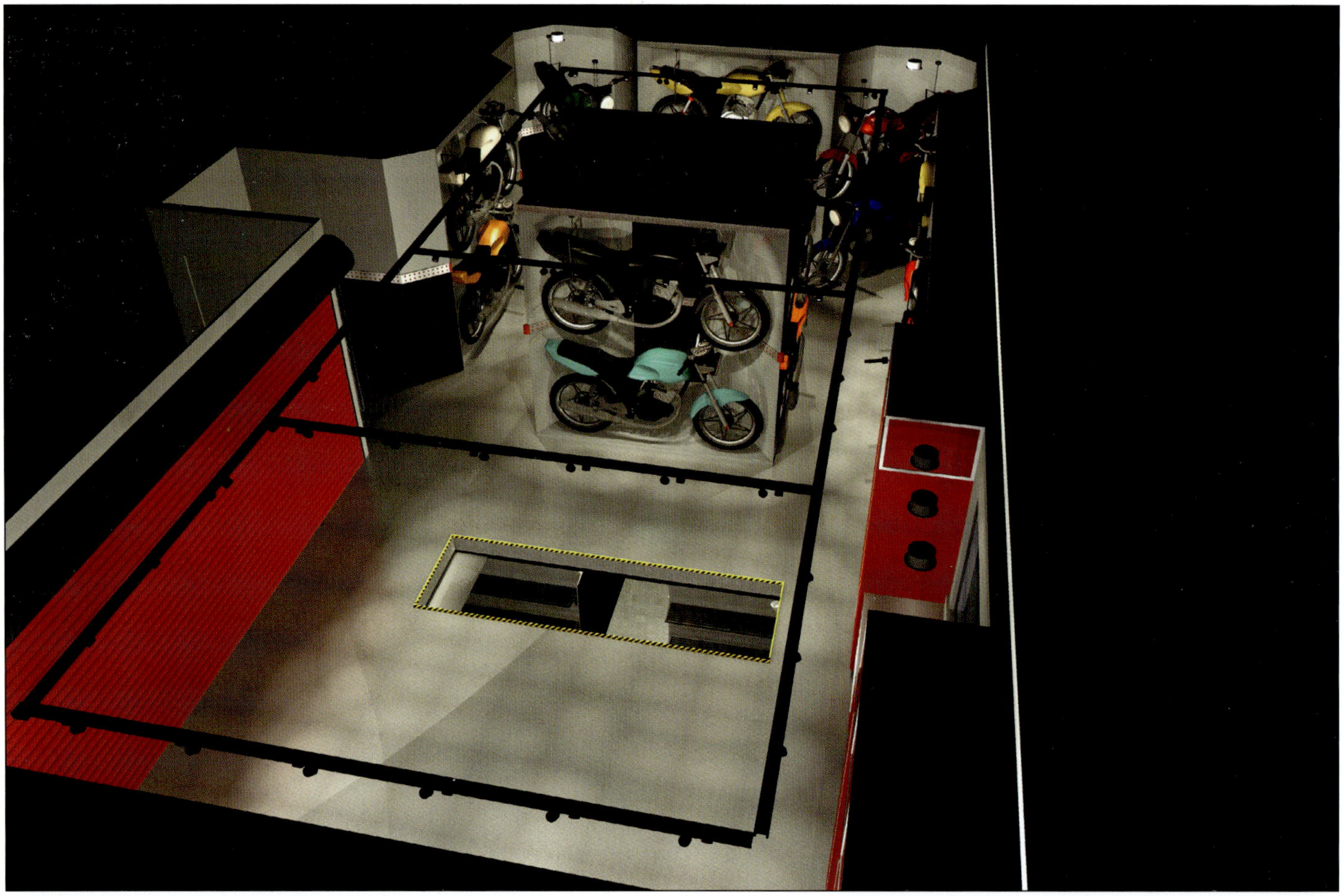

A computer-generated overhead perspective shows the mechanics bay and a display area for a dirt bike collector. *Courtesy of GarageMahals*

A specially designed oil pit is accessed via tunnel in a mechanic's bay. *Courtesy of GarageMahals*

A vintage gas station theme was perfect for an owner who collects. Retro in feel, this garage is beyond anything your grandfather dreamed of.
Courtesy of GarageMahals

GILMORE GASOLINE
GILMORE GASOLINE
GILMORE BLU-GREEN GASOLINE
Ask for— GILMORE 35¢
MOTOR OIL

Vintage gas pumps and cars glisten right along with the checkerboard floor and metallic doors.
Courtesy of GarageMahals

A Zen-inspired theme garage glows with warm colors and resounds with the melody of a waterfall cascading across cool green glass tile. The wet bar is paired with a waterfall for cool effect. *Courtesy of GarageMahals*

Gleaming chrome and mechanic's red balance the bronze metallic floor in this mechanic's dream garage, complete with a flat-screen television. *Courtesy of GarageMahals*

A garage sparkles in keeping with a treasured sports car collection. Textured metallic rubber wainscoting, a high-gloss bronze metallic floor, and other metallic finishes add to the inner glow of this Asian Art Deco inspired garage, nicknamed the "Zen" garage by the creator. Better than any drive-in theater, this venue features a wet bar flanked by water features. *Courtesy of Garage Mahals/ Photography: www.jessemoen.com*

Resources

All American Design & Furnishings, Inc
Folsom, California
916.919-3023
www.AllAmericanDesignandFurnishings.com

Aquatic Industries, Inc.
Leander, Texas
800-555-5324
www.aquaticwhirlpools.com

Architextures
Saint Louis, Missouri
314-961-9500
www.architexturesllc.com

Clopay Building Products
Mason, Ohio
513-770-4800
www.clopay.com

Cooper Garage Cabinet Systems
888-848-0059
www.thestampstore.com

diamondLife
412-793-3511
www.diamondlifegear.com

Fresh Air Screens
888-549-0783
www.freshairscreens.com

Garage Den
Frazer, Pennsylvania
610-889-0536
www.GarageDen.com

Garage Design Source
703-443-2608
www.GarageDesignSource.com

Garage Finisher, Inc.
Cleveland, Ohio
877-343-4743
www.garagefinisher.com

GarageMahals
Scottsdale, Arizona
602-315-4473
www.garagemahals.com

Garage Tek
866-664-2724
www.garagetek.com

Gregory Montillo
Framingham, Massachusetts
508-877-1676

Jeld-Wen Windows & Doors
800-535-3936
www.jeld-wen.com

One Day Floors
www.thestampstore.com
888-848-0059

OrganizIT
818-232-7683
www.organizitco.com

Premier Garage
610-358-9127
www.remiergarage.com

Rust-Oleum
800-323-3584
www.rustoleum.com

Vanguard Doors Sales & Service
Pennsburg, Pennsylvania
215-541-4848

Versatile Building Products, Inc.
800-535-3325
www.garagecoatings.com

More Schiffer Titles

www.schifferbooks.com

Wine Cellar Design. Tina Skinner. Over 300 images of wine cellars immerse you into the stylish and impressive world of today's vintage connoisseur. A wine cellar is becoming a standard feature of today's luxury home. The ability to invest in fine wines, to age them properly, and to have them on hand for entertaining is a luxury more people can afford. This book is packed with ideas and technical information for designing safe, stylish, beautiful wine cellars. Essays by leading designers and a section detailing the proper construction of a wine cellar make this an invaluable reference.
Size: 9" x 12" • 330 color photos, 25 illustrations • 256 pp.
ISBN: 978-0-7643-2862-6 • hard cover • $49.95

Wine Cellars: An Exploration of Stylish Storage. Tina Skinner & Melissa Cardona. This thorough and inspiring book provides a vicarious tour of the best in wine bottle storage. Visit more than 100 absolutely stunning, private wine cellars in over 200 beautiful color photographs. Peruse racking systems, tasting tables, and artful touches, created by leading wine cellar designers, including Paul Wyatt, Kathleen Valentini, Gary LaRose, and Doug Smith.

Additionally, this is a guidebook to wine cellars in some of the world's most renowned hotels and restaurants, where private parties can reserve a table and dine amidst coveted vintages. The book also visits handsome displays in restaurants that showcase wine programs to customers.

The result is thousands of wonderful ideas for wine storage and display. This is the first work of its kind, making it an invaluable guide for architects, designers, and discerning homeowners and restaurateurs.
Size: 11" x 8 1/2" • 200+ color photos • 160 pp.
ISBN: 0-7643-1965-5 • hard cover • $49.95

Making Concrete Countertops. Buddy Rhodes with Susan Andrews. For the first time, the art and craft of creating concrete countertops is detailed, step-by-step. This invaluable manual will guide craftsmen through each step of creating a cast concrete countertop, from the careful process of measuring for a template, to building a mold, through casting and installation. Moreover, you will be inspired by a gallery of more than 60 color images that explore actual kitchens and baths featuring hand-crafted countertops.

With more than 30 years of experience in concrete art and fabrication, artist Buddy Rhodes shares his skills and experience in this tell-all book. Most importantly, he shares the process he pioneered for creating the natural, stone-like pressed surface countertops that have become his hallmark. Additionally, he details techniques for hand-trowelled and polished countertop surfaces.

As the popularity of concrete in home decor soars, this book will be an indespensable guide for any craftsman who hopes to make his mark in this expanding market. Amateurs alike will appreciate the intricate detail and the helpful hints that Rhodes includes in this comprehensive guide.

Size: 8-1/2" x 11" • 472 color photos • 144 pp.

ISBN: 0-7643-2477-2 • hard cover • $39.95

Making Concrete Countertops with Buddy Rhodes: Advanced Techniques. Buddy Rhodes with Susan Andrews. The companion volume to Making Concrete Countertops with Buddy Rhodes, this book details the art and craft of creating vertical concrete applications as well as integral sink and drainboard elements and curved-edge counters, for advanced users of the medium. An invaluable manual for contractors, architects, and expert handypersons alike, the project photography within will guide you step-by-step in the creation of an outdoor kitchen project, from the careful process of measuring a template, to building a mold, to casting, curing, and installation.

With more than 30 years of experience in concrete art and fabrication, artist Buddy Rhodes shares his skills and experience in this useful, practical book. Most importantly, he shares the process he pioneered for creating the natural, stone-like pressed surfaces that have become his hallmark.

As the popularity of concrete in home decor soars, this book will be an indispensable guide for any craftsman who hopes to make his mark on this incredible, expanding market.

Size: 8 1/2" x 11" • 432 color photos • 144 pp.

ISBN: 978-0-7643-3014-8 • hard cover • $39.99

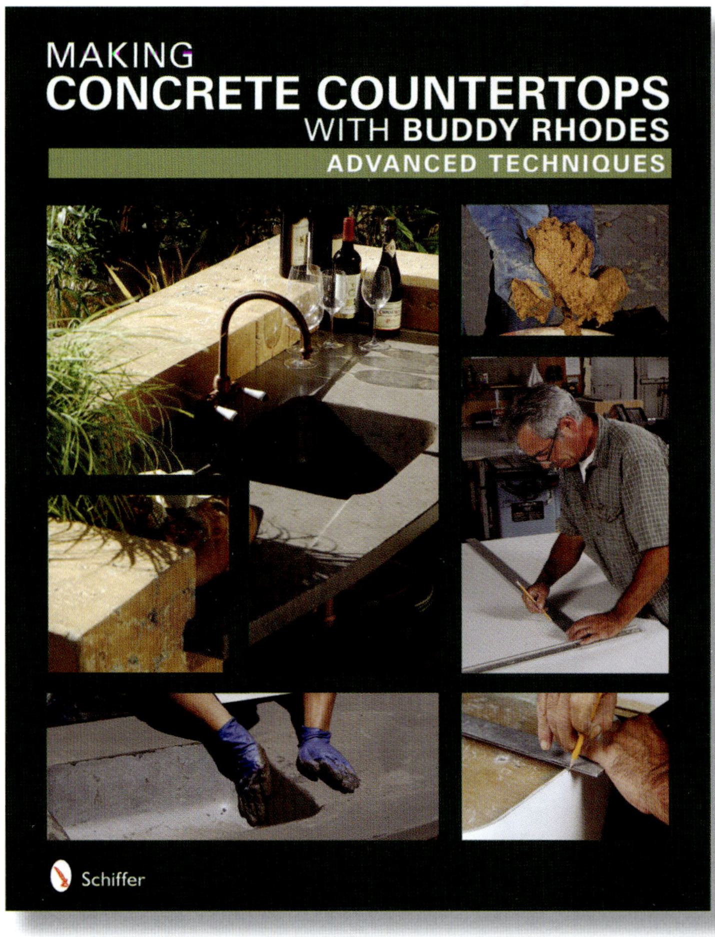

Home Office, Library, and Den Design. Tina Skinner. Visit more than 200 private offices, dens, and libraries with ideas for floor layouts, paneling and shelving systems, storage systems, and color schemes. Work by leading architects and designers, as well as practical turn-key setups from manufacturers are represented, along with contact information to help you design and furnish your perfect office, library, or den.
Size: 8 1/2" x 11" • 242 color • 144 pp.
ISBN: 0-7643-1842-X • soft cover • $24.95

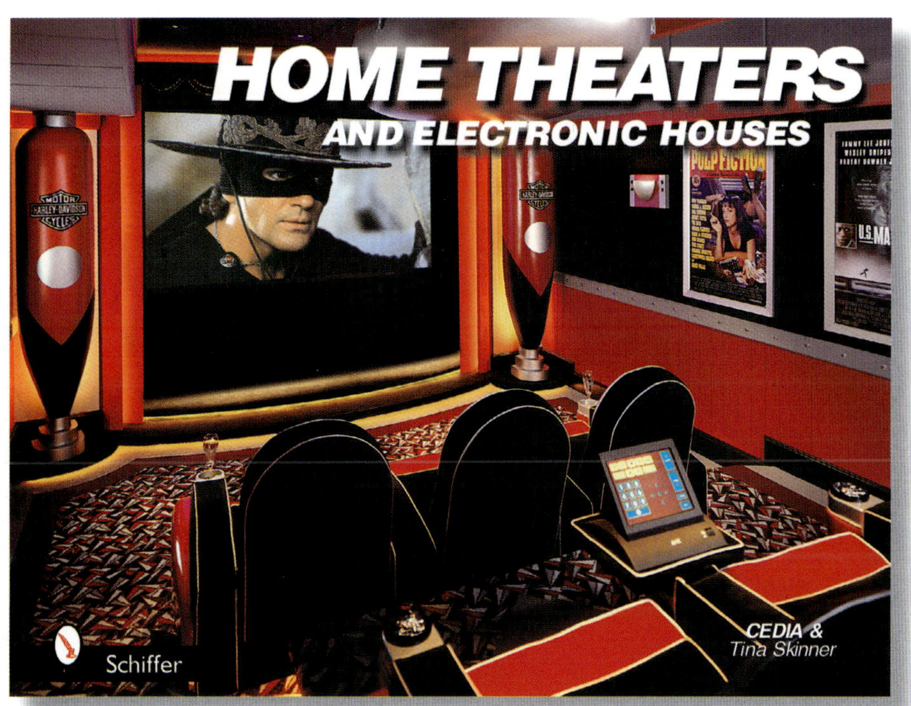

Home Theaters and Electronic Houses. CEDIA & Tina Skinner. A colorful tour of sound-proofed, silver-screened retreats fit for movie stars, Starship commanders, and sultans. Visit amazing home theaters and high-tech homes, where room-by-room sensors and touch-pad controls put lighting, sound, temperature, and security at your command. Watch screens descend or ascend from unexpected hiding places, projectors appear, and windows disappear in James-Bond like mechanical transitions. And enjoy flat-screen and plasma entertainments in the most unexpected of places -- shower stalls, pool rooms, home sports bars, and more, tucked into basements, spare bedrooms, playrooms, garages, and even attics. Includes equipment lists for many of the projects, an essay on the art of wiring complicated entertainment and whole-house projects, and another essay offering advice on choosing a professional to help you transform your home.
Size: 11" x 8 1/2" • 230+ color photos • 176 pp.
ISBN: 0-7643-1957-4 • hard cover • $44.95

Power Rooms: Executive Offices, Corporate Lobbies, and Conference Rooms. Jack Neith. Look into America's most notable corporate atriums, boardrooms, lobbies, seating areas, and executive offices and experience their powerful interior designs. Actual installations by professional architects and designers, these spaces reflect the powerful atmosphere in which corporate decisions are made daily. Over 235 color photographs present a cross-section of corporate designs and contemporary rooms that are on the cutting edge. The rooms use various materials, colors, light, and structural containment to provide ambiance. Some are simple designs utilizing creativity and function as their inspiration, while others use bolder elements to create memorable designs. From wood to polished marble and accent lighting, the elements add drama to the space. This book will provide awe and inspiration to executives, architects, interior designers, and committee members looking for powerful ideas.
Size: 11" x 8 1/2" • 238 color photos • 160 pp.
ISBN: 978-0-7643-2920-3 • hard cover • $49.95

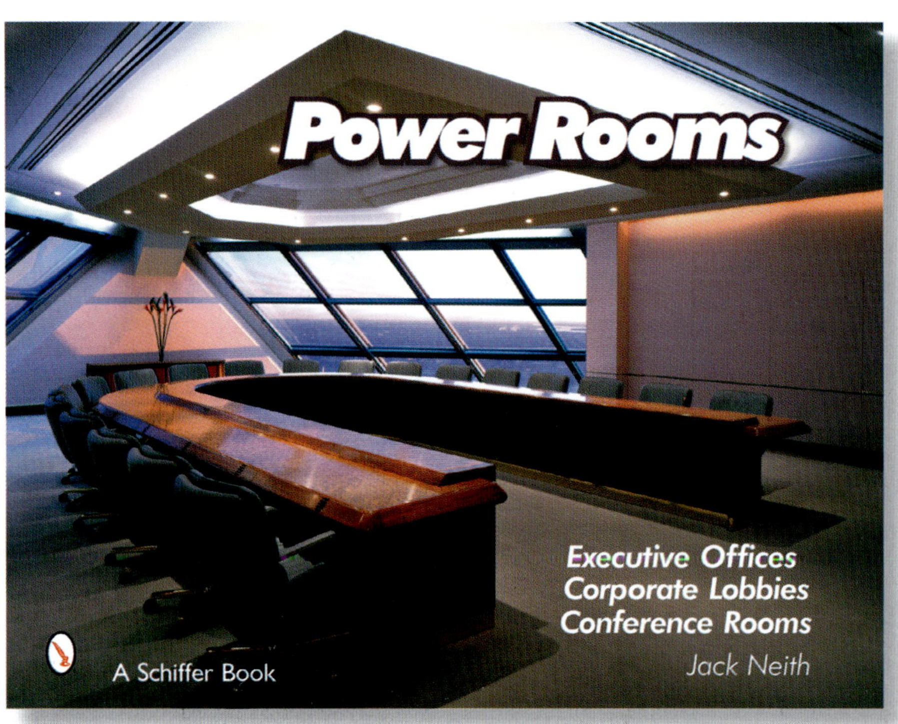

Schiffer books may be ordered from your local bookstore, or they may be ordered directly from the publisher by writing to:

Schiffer Publishing Ltd.
4880 Lower Valley Road
Atglen, PA 19310
Phone: (610) 593-1777; Fax: (610) 593-2002
E-mail: Info@schifferbooks.com

Please visit our web site catalog at:
www.schifferbooks.com
or write for a free catalog. Please include $5.00 for shipping and handling for the first two books and $2.00 for each additional book.
Free shipping for orders of $150 or more.

Printed in China